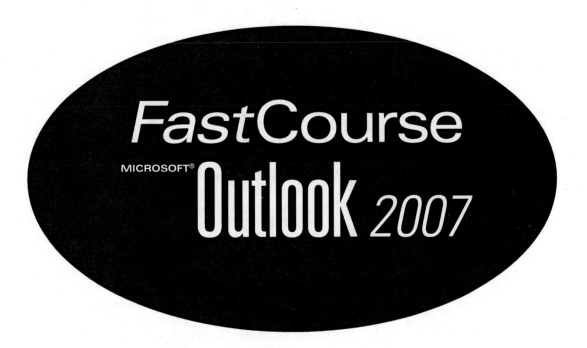

*Fast*Course

MICROSOFT®

Outlook *2007*

Judy Mardar

PC Source

LABYRINTH
L E A R N I N G ®

FastCourse Outlook 2007
by Judy Mardar

Copyright © 2009 by Labyrinth Learning

LABYRINTH
L E A R N I N G ®

Labyrinth Learning
PO Box 20818
El Sobrante, California 94820
800.522.9746
On the web at www.lablearning.com

President:
Brian Favro

Series Editor:
Russel Stolins

Acquisitions Editor:
Jason Favro

Managing Editor:
Laura A. Lionello

Production Manager:
Rad Proctor

Editorial/Production Team:
Belinda Breyer, Alyssa Favro, Alec Fehl,
Alona Harris, Sandy Jones, and Arl S. Nadel

Indexing: Joanne Sprott

Cover Illustration:
Béatrice Favereau

Cover Design:
Seventeenth Street Studios

ITEM: 1-59136-240-7
ISBN-13: 978-1-59136-240-1

Manufactured in the United States of America.

10 9 8 7

FastCourse
Outlook 2007

Contents

LESSON 1 GETTING STARTED WITH OUTLOOK 2007   2

Introducing Outlook 2007   3
   Outlook Components   3
Starting Outlook   4
Navigating the Outlook Screen   5
   Use the Navigation Pane   5
   Personalize the Reading Pane   7
   Explore the Ribbon   9
Getting Help   10
   Where to Get Help   10
   Print Help Topics   12
Concepts Review   13

LESSON 2 WORKING WITH EMAIL   14

Getting Started with Outlook Email   15
   Setting Email Options   15
   Types of Email Accounts   15
   View Settings on an Email Account   15
   Check for New Messages   16
Sending Messages   18
   Multiple Recipients   18
   Use Signatures to Save Time   20
   Insert a Signature in a Message   22
   Attaching Files   24
   Spell Check   26
Handling Incoming Messages   29
   Send/Receive Button   29
   Check Individual Accounts for Messages   29
   Read Messages   30
   Respond to Messages   32
   Print Messages   34
Organizing Your Messages   35
   Understand the Folder List   35
   Creating Folders   35
   Move a Message to a Folder   36
   Delete Messages   38
   Archive Messages   39
Concepts Review   40

LESSON 3 WORKING WITH CONTACT INFORMATION   42

Managing Contact Information   43
   View the Contacts List   43
Working with Contacts   44
   Create a Contact in the Contacts Window   44
   Add the Sender of an Incoming Message to Contacts   44
   Edit Contacts   46
   Sort the Contacts List   47
   Send Messages to Contacts   47
Working with Distribution Lists   49
   Creating Distribution Lists   49
   Send Messages to Groups   50
   Revise a Distribution List   52
Concepts Review   53

LESSON 4 USING THE CALENDAR   54

Working with Appointments   55
   Schedule an Appointment   55
   Edit Appointments   56
   Set a Reminder for an Appointment   57
   Invite Attendees   57
Recurring Appointments   59
   Editing Recurring Appointments   60
Exploring the Calendar   62
   Day View   63
   Week View   63
   Month View   63
   Change Calendar Options   65
Sharing Calendars   66
   Custom Calendars   66
   Share Your Calendar through Email   69
   Open a Calendar Received via Email   71
Printing Calendars   73
   Use Page Setup   74
Concepts Review   75

LESSON 5 USING NOTES, TASKS, AND THE JOURNAL 76

Working with Notes	77
Creating a Note	77
Copy a Note onto the Desktop	77
Working with Tasks	79
Navigating Tasks	79
Creating a Task	80
Editing Tasks	82
Set a Reminder	82
Assigning Tasks	83
Accept or Decline a Task	85
Using the Journal	86
Setting Journal Options	86
Create a Journal Entry	87
Viewing Journal Entries	88
Concepts Review	91
Index	*92*

Getting Started with Outlook 2007

In this lesson, you will become familiar with the basics of Outlook 2007. You will learn to navigate the Outlook screen, and you will observe the various methods available for getting help. Learning these skills early will provide you with a solid foundation to make you comfortable maneuvering around Outlook and will prepare you for learning the features introduced in later lessons.

LESSON OBJECTIVES

After studying this lesson, you will be able to:

- Identify Outlook components
- Start the Outlook program
- Navigate the Outlook screen
- Get help on Outlook topics

LESSON TIMING

- Concepts/Hands-On: 1 hr 00 min
- Concepts Review: 15 min
- Total: 1 hr 15 min

CASE STUDY: GETTING TO KNOW OUTLOOK

After many years as a stay-at-home mom, Brett Conley is returning to the workforce as an administrative assistant. She was told during the interview that her new company uses Microsoft Outlook 2007 as their electronic communication tool. Since she has never used a program such as Outlook before, Brett wants to take a look at what the program offers and feel comfortable navigating the screen. Most important to Brett before she shows up for her first day and continues to familiarize herself with Outlook is to know how to find help when she needs it.

Additional learning resources are available at labpub.com/learn/outlook07_fastcourse1/

Introducing Outlook 2007

Microsoft Outlook is a program that allows you to send and receive electronic mail (email), maintain an address book of all of your contacts, have a place to enter personal appointments and tasks, set up meetings with others, and keep you organized by reminding you of all you need to do.

Outlook Components

The following is a brief overview of the five major components of Outlook.

- **Electronic mail (email):** This is the component that allows you to send and receive email messages with or without a file attached to them. You can save emails in separate folders to keep them organized, rather than keeping all incoming messages in the Inbox and all outgoing messages in the Sent Items folder.

- **Contacts:** This is where you keep contact information—such as names, street addresses, phone numbers, email addresses, etc.—for all of the people with whom you communicate. Distribution lists can come in handy when a group of people is required to receive the same information (for example, messages sent regularly to department managers only).

- **Calendar:** Calendars allow you to keep track of personal appointments, including those that recur at regular intervals. You can also choose to share a calendar with others while keeping certain items private. You can also use a calendar to remind yourself when it's time to do an activity.

- **Tasks:** No more little yellow sticky notes needed. All of those things you need to do, people to call, things to buy, and so forth can now be added as tasks. You can assign dates and reminders to your tasks and then mark them complete as you finish them. Outlook includes a To-Do Bar that displays your Tasks list, which is linked to your calendar; everything you need to do for the day is right there in front of you.

- **Notes:** This piece of Outlook lets you store miscellaneous information that doesn't necessarily require a due date or a reminder. For example, you may decide to store a list of accounts numbers or "cheat sheets" on various procedures you need to accomplish. This is the perfect, safe place to store them—instead of trying to keep track of those nasty sticky notes that always seem to disappear.

Starting Outlook

The method you use to start Outlook is your personal preference. You can use either the Start menu or a shortcut icon. Depending on which version of Windows you are using and how Microsoft Office was installed on your computer, your screen or procedure may differ slightly. For example, in Windows XP Classic view, the command on the Start menu is Programs (rather than All Programs). To launch Outlook, use one of the following methods. Once it opens, you may begin working with any of the Outlook components.

Note: Screen captures in this book are shown using the Windows Classic theme. Your screen may differ slightly depending on your installation of Outlook and Windows.

■ Click the **start** button and choose Microsoft Office→Microsoft Outlook 2007 from the All Programs menu.

■ Click the Outlook button on the Quick Launch toolbar at the bottom of the screen near the Start button.

■ Double-click the Outlook shortcut button on the Windows Desktop.

Hands-On 1.1   Start Outlook

1. Click the **start** button and choose All Programs.

2. Position your mouse pointer on the Microsoft Office submenu ▶ button and choose Microsoft Outlook 2007.

3. Choose No if you are asked about synchronizing RSS Feeds.

4. Click the Maximize button to make the Outlook window fill the entire screen, if necessary.

Navigating the Outlook Screen

The Outlook screen contains several sections with content that changes depending on which Outlook component is selected. On the left of the Outlook window is the Navigation pane, in the center is the Contents pane, and on the right is the To-Do Bar. The To-Do Bar can be displayed or hidden by minimizing or maximizing it. When maximized, the To-Do Bar displays the current calendar and any appointments or tasks for the day.

The Standard toolbar displays buttons for frequently used commands. Different commands bring up different parts of the Ribbon, which you will learn about in the next section.

The menu bar in Outlook looks similar to the menu bar in other Office applications.

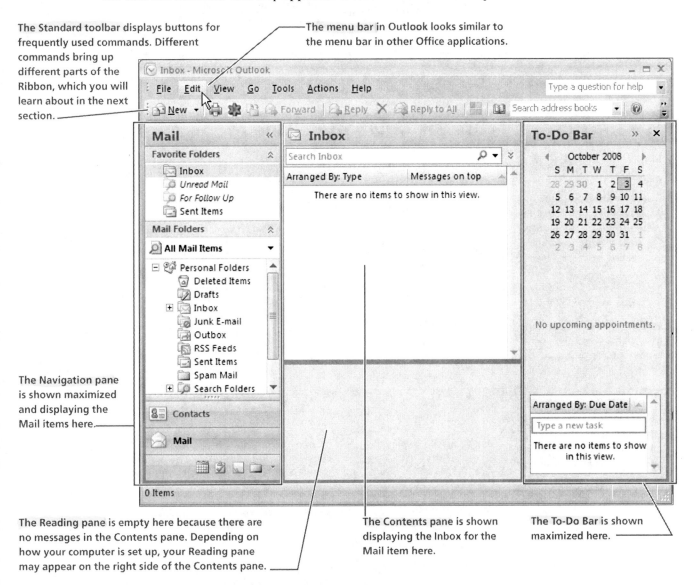

The Navigation pane is shown maximized and displaying the Mail items here.

The Reading pane is empty here because there are no messages in the Contents pane. Depending on how your computer is set up, your Reading pane may appear on the right side of the Contents pane.

The Contents pane is shown displaying the Inbox for the Mail item here.

The To-Do Bar is shown maximized here.

Use the Navigation Pane

The Navigation pane displays the contents of the selected Outlook component. When Mail is selected, the list of mail folders is displayed in the Navigation pane, while the list of messages appears in the Contents pane. Folders can contain subfolders to aid in organization. You will know that a folder contains a subfolder when you see a plus (+) sign next to the folder. You will learn more about folders in Lesson 2, Working with Email. When Contacts is selected, the Navigation pane displays a list of available views in which to view your contacts, while the

Contents pane displays the actual contact names. You can also control how items appear in the Navigation pane, such as displaying them in the list or simply as buttons at the bottom of the pane.

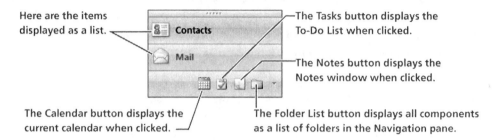

Here are the items displayed as a list.

The Tasks button displays the To-Do List when clicked.

The Notes button displays the Notes window when clicked.

The Calendar button displays the current calendar when clicked.

The Folder List button displays all components as a list of folders in the Navigation pane.

 Hands-On 1.2   Use the Navigation Pane

1. Follow these steps to use the Navigation pane:

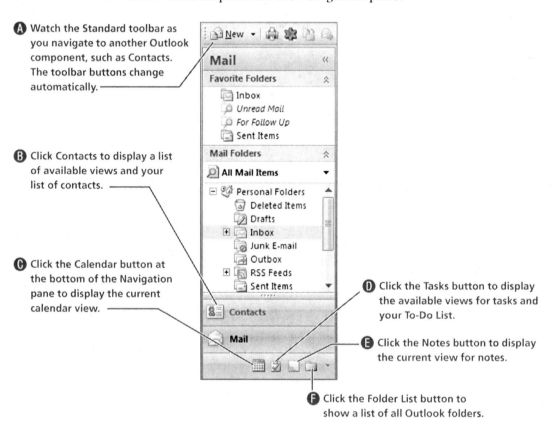

Ⓐ Watch the Standard toolbar as you navigate to another Outlook component, such as Contacts. The toolbar buttons change automatically.

Ⓑ Click Contacts to display a list of available views and your list of contacts.

Ⓒ Click the Calendar button at the bottom of the Navigation pane to display the current calendar view.

Ⓓ Click the Tasks button to display the available views for tasks and your To-Do List.

Ⓔ Click the Notes button to display the current view for notes.

Ⓕ Click the Folder List button to show a list of all Outlook folders.

2. Follow these steps to navigate your personal folders:

A Click the Deleted Items folder. Items you delete are held in this folder and are not immediately deleted from your computer.

B Click the Outbox folder. Items you send remain here until they are finished sending, at which time they appear in the Sent Items folder.

C Click the Mail button in the Navigation pane and then click Inbox.

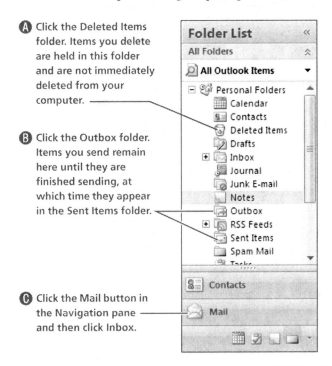

Personalize the Reading Pane

The Reading pane is the section of the screen that displays the actual contents of the selected item in the Contents pane. For example, when a message in the Sent Items folder is selected, the Reading pane displays the actual verbiage of the message. The Reading pane can be displayed to the right of or below the Contents pane. It can also be resized to your personal preference.

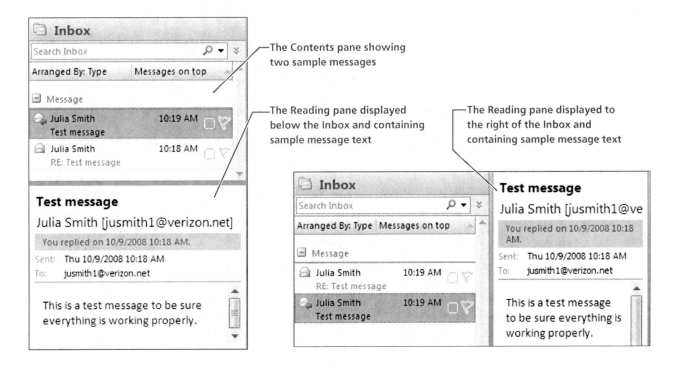

The Contents pane showing two sample messages

The Reading pane displayed below the Inbox and containing sample message text

The Reading pane displayed to the right of the Inbox and containing sample message text

Hands-On 1.3   Personalize the Reading Pane

1. Follow these steps to display the Reading pane to the right of the Contents pane:

Ⓐ Click View on the menu bar to display the list of View commands and subcommands.

Ⓑ Point to the Reading Pane submenu to display its commands.

Ⓒ Click Right to display the Reading pane to the right of the Contents pane.

2. Choose View→Reading Pane→Bottom to place the Reading pane below the Contents pane.

3. Follow these steps to resize the Reading pane:

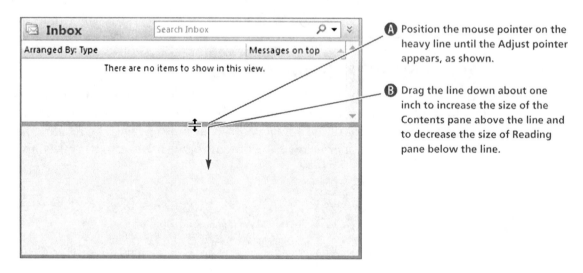

Ⓐ Position the mouse pointer on the heavy line until the Adjust pointer appears, as shown.

Ⓑ Drag the line down about one inch to increase the size of the Contents pane above the line and to decrease the size of Reading pane below the line.

4. Choose View→Reading Pane→Right.

5. Follow these steps to resize the Reading pane when it's displayed on the right:

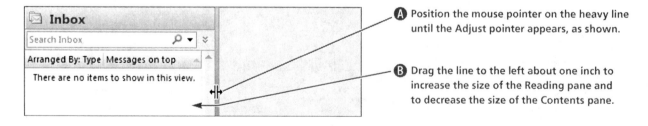

Ⓐ Position the mouse pointer on the heavy line until the Adjust pointer appears, as shown.

Ⓑ Drag the line to the left about one inch to increase the size of the Reading pane and to decrease the size of the Contents pane.

6. Move the Reading pane back to the bottom of the Contents pane.

Explore the Ribbon

Each section of the Ribbon contains related actions for a specific command. For example, when you click the New button on the Outlook toolbar, the Ribbon displays groups of actions related to creating a new message. It is further broken down into related actions and grouped by contextual tabs across the top of the Ribbon. The contextual tabs appear depending on what choices you make and the buttons, which are displayed by command group names at the bottom of the Ribbon, change depending on the tab selected. For example, on the New command section of the Ribbon, you can display the underlying Insert actions to gain access to the Attach File command. You will use the Ribbon in all of the remaining lessons.

Clicking the New button opens the section of the Ribbon that contains commands used when creating new messages. ——

New Message contextual tab on the Ribbon

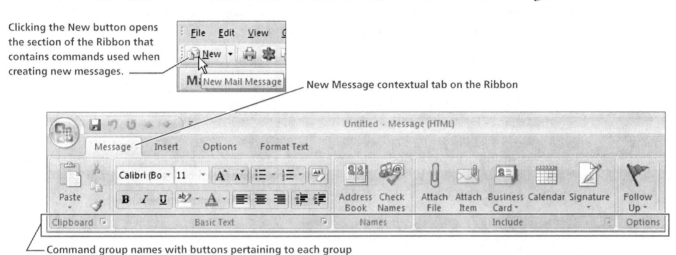

——— Command group names with buttons pertaining to each group

 Hands-On 1.4   **View the Insert Contextual Tab**

1. Click the New button.

2. Follow these steps to open a dialog box using the Ribbon:

Ⓐ Click the Insert tab to display the Insert tab group of commands. ——

Ⓑ Click the Attach File button.

3. Click the Cancel button when the Insert File dialog box opens.

4. Click the Close ⊠ button on the Untitled - Message window.

Getting Help

Microsoft Office provides a complete reference book at your fingertips. You can get the help you need for just about any Outlook topic immediately with just a few clicks. In addition to Outlook's built-in Help system, the Microsoft Office website offers further Help options.

Where to Get Help

There are several methods to find the help you need. All topics are linked to keywords that help identify them. For example, getting help on printing email messages can be located by using the keyword "print" in your search method. Once you receive your results, you can leave the results window open or you can print the instructions.

Browse for Help

Outlook's Help window displays a list of major topics through which you can browse. (This is a great learning tool when you have any free time. Just start browsing; you'll be surprised at how much you'll learn.) When you click one of the topic links, a list of related subcategories and finally your step-by-step instructions will appear. You can also type a keyword in the Search box whenever the Outlook Help window is open. You can move backward and forward between topics or display the topic list as a table of contents, all by using the Help toolbar buttons.

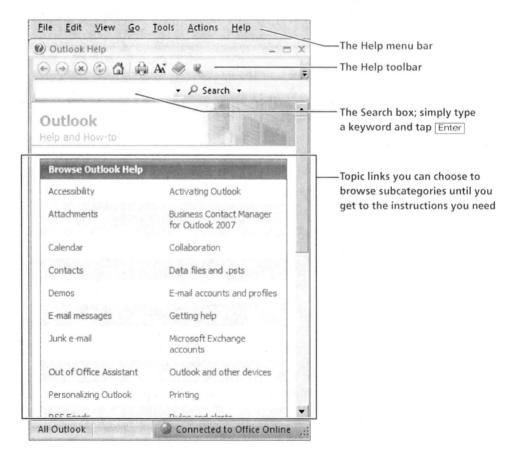

Displaying the Help window can be accomplished with any of the following methods:

- Click the Office Help 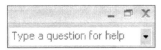 button on the Standard toolbar.
- Choose Help→Microsoft Office Outlook Help on the menu bar.
- Press F1.

Ask a Simple Question

If you have a question about using Outlook, you can type it in the Type a Question for Help box located in the upper-right corner of the Outlook screen. Best of all, you don't need to know all of Outlook's technical terminology! You can type your question in plain English. Outlook Help is very intuitive and will display several results with topics closely related to your question.

Hands-On 1.5   Get Help

1. Choose Help→Microsoft Office Outlook Help on the menu bar.

2. Follow these steps to browse for help on creating a new message:

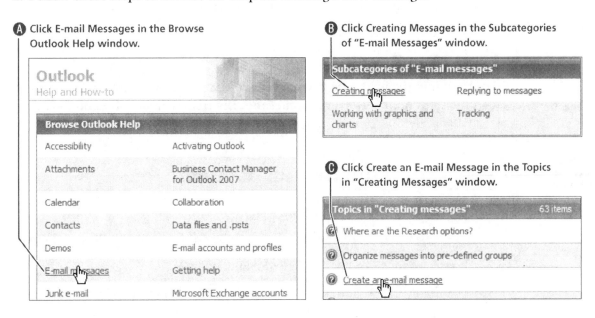

3. Scroll down to read the instructions on creating a new email message.

4. Follow these steps to search for instructions on printing help topics:

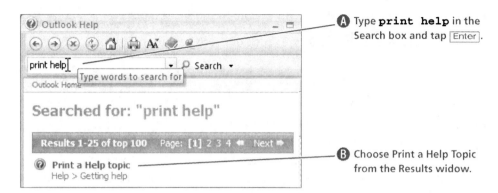

Ⓐ Type **print help** in the Search box and tap Enter.

Ⓑ Choose Print a Help Topic from the Results widow.

5. Click the Close ☒ button on the Outlook Help window.

6. Type **how do I reply to a message** in the Type a Question for Help box and tap Enter.

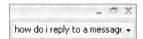

7. Choose Reply to or Forward a Message in the Results window.

8. Scroll down to read the Reply to the Sender topic. When you're finished, close Help.

Print Help Topics

Once you find the instructions you need, you can choose to leave the results window open and read the steps online. However, sometimes the Help window takes up too much room. Thus, it is usually preferable to print a hard copy of the instructions.

 Hands-On 1.6   Print Help Instructions

1. Click the Office Help 🔘 button.

2. Type **create a contact** in the Search box of the Help window and tap Enter.

3. Choose Create a Contact from the Results window.

4. Click the Print 🖨 button on the Outlook Help toolbar to print the instructions.

5. Close the Help window.

Concepts Review

True/False Questions

1. There are only two major components in Outlook: email and the calendar.   TRUE   ~~FALSE~~

2. You read your messages in the Contents pane.   TRUE   ~~FALSE~~

3. When the To-Do Bar is maximized, it displays appointments and tasks for the day.   ~~TRUE~~   FALSE

4. The Reading pane can be placed to the right or below the Contents pane.   ~~TRUE~~   FALSE

5. The Reading pane shows the contents of all Outlook components.   TRUE   ~~FALSE~~

6. You can assign dates and reminders to tasks.   ~~TRUE~~   FALSE

7. Contextual tabs on the Ribbon contain related actions for specific commands.   ~~TRUE~~   FALSE

8. You can print a hard copy of a Help topic.   ~~TRUE~~   FALSE

9. The Navigation pane displays a list of your messages.   TRUE   ~~FALSE~~

10. You can get help by typing keywords or browsing topics.   ~~TRUE~~   FALSE

Multiple Choice Questions

1. Which command is used to display the Reading pane below the Contents pane?
   a. Format→Reading Pane→Below
   b. View→Reading Pane→Below
   c. Tools→Reading Pane→Bottom
   d. View→Reading Pane→Bottom

2. Which item on the Navigation pane do you use to display your list of email addresses?
   a. Address book
   b. Contacts
   c. Distribution list
   d. Folder list

3. Which Outlook component should you use to remind yourself of people to call or items to buy at the store?
   a. Contacts
   b. Notes
   c. Tasks
   d. Email

4. Which is *not* a way to get help in Outlook?
   a. Go to the Microsoft Office website.
   b. Choose Help→Microsoft Office Outlook Help.
   c. Choose Tools→Help→Microsoft Office Outlook Help.
   d. Type a keyword in the Search box.

LESSON 2

Working with Email

In today's personal and professional world, email has become the standard, acceptable, and very easy way to communicate across your office and across the world. You can send and receive messages, documents, pictures, music, and videos. In this lesson, you will be introduced briefly to the different types of email; how to set email options; how to send, read, reply to, and forward messages; and how to keep your email organized.

LESSON OBJECTIVES

After studying this lesson, you will be able to:

- Set email options
- Send messages
- Handle incoming messages
- Organize your Inbox

LESSON TIMING

- Concepts/Hands-On: 2 hrs 30 min
- Concepts Review: 15 min
- Total: 2 hrs 45 min

CASE STUDY: GETTING A HANDLE ON EMAIL BASICS

John Smith is the sales manager for M-Line Brake Company. All personnel have learned that they will begin using Microsoft Outlook next week. John isn't too worried because he's been using a webmail account to communicate with his son, who's away at college, for some time now. He knows that there will be a transition period for learning Outlook, but he's comfortable with the challenge. John deals with distributors all across the United States, and he will be sending reports and general correspondence to them and his sales staff. Up until now, John has kept folders in a physical file cabinet for each distributor. Now he will learn how to maintain that same organization with his electronic documents.

Additional learning resources are available at labpub.com/learn/outlook07_fastcourse1/

Getting Started with Outlook Email

Out of all the Outlook components, email is the most widely used. It has become the standard means of communicating in the business world—and it has certainly grown in popularity in our personal lives as well. Email is nearly as simple to use as the telephone and is an easy way to communicate, especially when you are busy. For example, when you use the telephone, you pick up the receiver and dial a number, and then, before you actually get down to the business at hand, you usually feel the need to exchange some pleasantries. All of this takes up your precious time. However, when you send an email, you address it, type a subject, type your message, and send it on its way.

Setting Email Options

There are many email options available in Outlook. This course will cover a couple of the most popular ones, namely adding a signature to your messages and having Outlook check for new messages automatically.

Types of Email Accounts

There are different sources from where you get email accounts: your company, an Internet service provider (ISP), or maybe more familiar to you, a webmail account such as Yahoo! Mail, Gmail, or Hotmail. An important fact to understand is that Outlook does not create or supply you with an email account; it merely provides you with *access* to your accounts.

View Settings on an Email Account

Settings required for your email account to work include user information, server information, and login information. Whatever you enter in the Your Name field of the User Information section is the name your recipients will see when you send them email. The email address contains a username and domain name. In the email address jsmith@anycorp.com, "jsmith" is the username and "anycorp.com" is the domain name. Your ISP or the network adminis-trator at your office will tell you which kind of account you are using, plus supply you with other configuration details necessary to set up your account properly.

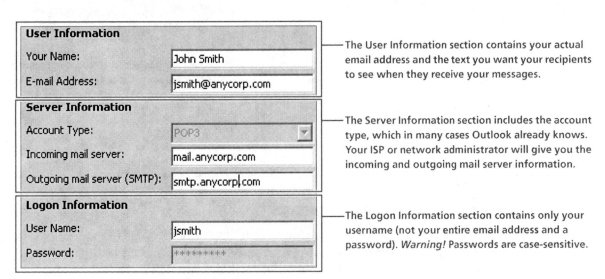

The User Information section contains your actual email address and the text you want your recipients to see when they receive your messages.

The Server Information section includes the account type, which in many cases Outlook already knows. Your ISP or network administrator will give you the incoming and outgoing mail server information.

The Logon Information section contains only your username (not your entire email address and a password). *Warning!* Passwords are case-sensitive.

On the
Web

Before You Begin: If your computer does not have an email account set up, you will perform the exercises as a web-based simulation (WebSim). Whenever you see the On the Web icon, you will be working as if you were actually using Microsoft Outlook; however, the exercise is actually being performed on a web page. Begin with step 1 below.

If you do have an email account set up, skip steps 1 and 2 and begin the exercise with step 3 below.

1. Start Internet Explorer and navigate to the student web page for this book (labpub.com/learn/outlook07_fastcourse1).

2. Click the link for Hands-On 2.1 Change Your Name in Account Settings.

3. Choose Tools→Account Settings in the menu bar.

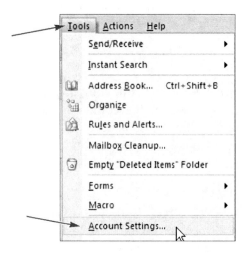

4. Follow these steps to change your name in the User Information section:

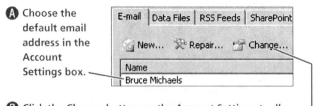

Ⓐ Choose the default email address in the Account Settings box.

Ⓑ Click the Change button on the Account Settings toolbar.

Ⓒ In the Your Name box, replace the sample text with **[your name]**. *Do not* change any other settings.

5. Click Next and then Finish.

6. Click Close.

Check for New Messages

Until John gets into the habit of remembering to check for new messages, he should consider setting an option to check for them at regular intervals and then notify him when they have arrived—one less thing for him to remember to do. You will learn how to check for messages manually in the Handling Incoming Messages section later in this lesson. The time interval to check for messages can be anywhere from one minute up to twenty-four hours (that's 1,440 minutes). Some people like to check for messages very frequently, while others can go a half-hour or so. It's purely a personal decision.

Depending on how busy the mail servers are on the sending and receiving ends, a message may arrive very quickly or after several minutes. Still, using email is a whole lot faster than putting a stamp on an envelope and throwing it in a mailbox!

 Hands-On 2.2   **Set the Option to Check for New Messages**

 If your computer does not have an email account set up, begin with step 1 below and perform the WebSim online. Otherwise, skip step 1 and begin this exercise with step 2.

1. Go to **labpub.com/learn/outlook07_fastcourse1** and click the link for Hands-On 2.2 Set the Option to Check for New Messages.

2. Choose Tools→Options in the menu bar.

3. Follow these steps to set the time interval:

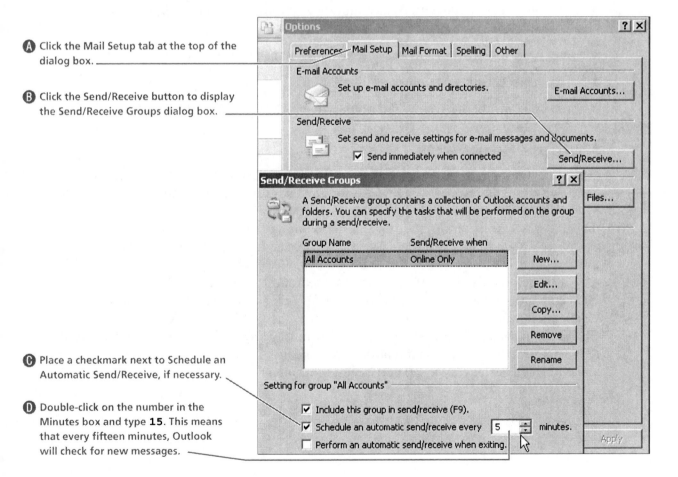

Ⓐ Click the Mail Setup tab at the top of the dialog box.

Ⓑ Click the Send/Receive button to display the Send/Receive Groups dialog box.

Ⓒ Place a checkmark next to Schedule an Automatic Send/Receive, if necessary.

Ⓓ Double-click on the number in the Minutes box and type **15**. This means that every fifteen minutes, Outlook will check for new messages.

4. Click Close and then OK.

Sending Messages

Although you learned in Lesson 1, Getting Started with Outlook 2007, about all of the components available in Outlook, the fact remains that the majority of people who use Outlook use it to send and receive email messages. John is pleased at what he has learned so far, and he is feeling very comfortable about the prospect of sending messages. He has learned that you can start to fill in the header boxes at the top by either clicking in them or tapping the [Tab] key to move around them. Once an address has been entered, Outlook remembers it. So, the next time you begin typing the first few letters of it in an address box, a list of addresses beginning with those letters appears.

There are a few rules and email etiquette issues to point out. Some of the do's and don'ts include the following:

- Don't use spaces in an email address; it just won't work. All email addresses must follow the same format: username@domainname.com.

- Do summarize your message in the subject. This makes it easy for your recipients to keep their messages organized.

- Don't type in all capital letters, as tempting as it may be. This is interpreted as yelling. It also makes the text more difficult to read.

- Don't write anything in a message that you wouldn't be comfortable saying in public.

- Do use correct capitalization and punctuation.

- Do type a semicolon between multiple recipients in the address boxes.

Multiple Recipients

A message can be sent to one or many recipients. When a message is sent to multiple recipients, everyone that receives it will see the address of everyone to whom it was sent if the addresses are entered in the To box. Thus, if you don't want everyone knowing to whom the message was sent, enter the addresses in the Blind Carbon Copy (Bcc) box instead. If the Bcc box is not displayed in a new message box, you can add it using the Ribbon. You will learn more about the Ribbon later in this lesson. When all recipients are in the Bcc box, each one only sees their own address. If some names are in the To and Carbon Copy (Cc) boxes, the Bcc recipients can see those addresses also, but the people in the To and Cc cannot see the Bcc recipients. A general rule for placing an address in the Cc box as opposed to the To box is that the people in the Cc box are only receiving the message for informational purposes. That is, they have no action to take, and typically are not expected to reply. Multiple email addresses in any of the address boxes are separated with semicolons.

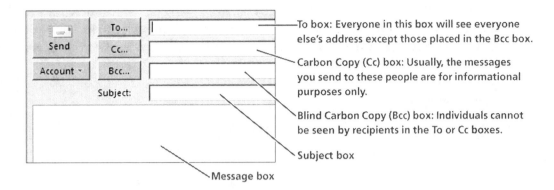

To box: Everyone in this box will see everyone else's address except those placed in the Bcc box.

Carbon Copy (Cc) box: Usually, the messages you send to these people are for informational purposes only.

Blind Carbon Copy (Bcc) box: Individuals cannot be seen by recipients in the To or Cc boxes.

Subject box

Message box

 Hands-On 2.3   **Create New Messages**

 On the Web

If your computer does not have an email account set up, begin with step 1 below and perform the WebSim online. Otherwise, skip step 1 and begin this exercise with step 2.

1. Go to **labpub.com/learn/outlook07_fastcourse1** and click the link for Hands-On 2.3 Create New Messages.

2. Click the New button on the toolbar to open a new message window.

3. Follow these steps to add a Bcc box to the message window:

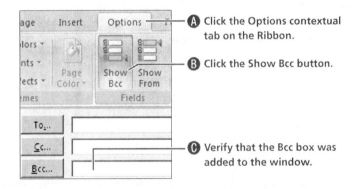

Ⓐ Click the Options contextual tab on the Ribbon.

Ⓑ Click the Show Bcc button.

Ⓒ Verify that the Bcc box was added to the window.

4. Follow these steps to create a message:

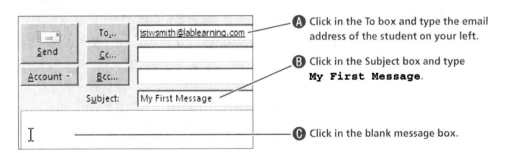

Ⓐ Click in the To box and type the email address of the student on your left.

Ⓑ Click in the Subject box and type **My First Message**.

Ⓒ Click in the blank message box.

5. Type the following text in the Message box, tapping [Enter] only where indicated:

I am seeing just how easy it is to work in Outlook. Creating my first email message is a breeze. I think I'm going to love this program. [Enter]
[Enter]
[Your Name]

6. Click the [Send] button in the new message window.

7. Click the [New] button.

8. Follow these steps to complete the header section of the message box:

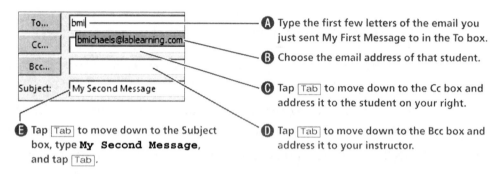

Ⓐ Type the first few letters of the email you just sent My First Message to in the To box.

Ⓑ Choose the email address of that student.

Ⓒ Tap [Tab] to move down to the Cc box and address it to the student on your right.

Ⓓ Tap [Tab] to move down to the Bcc box and address it to your instructor.

Ⓔ Tap [Tab] to move down to the Subject box, type **My Second Message**, and tap [Tab].

9. Type the following message:

My first message was easy, too. I think I'll try sending a new one to more than one person. How hard can it be, anyway? [Enter]
[Enter]
[Your Name]

10. Click the [Send] button.

Use Signatures to Save Time

A signature is the text you enter at the end of a message (your name, title, company, and so forth). Since John will be sending many messages, he will create a signature that Outlook will store and keep ready for him to insert at any time. John can also designate a signature to be inserted automatically into each message he responds to or creates.

Some messages John writes are not for business purposes. He has learned from a colleague that Outlook allows him to save multiple signatures and will display the list of signatures from which to insert manually.

1. Choose Tools→Options from the menu bar.

2. Follow these steps to display the Signatures and Stationery dialog box:

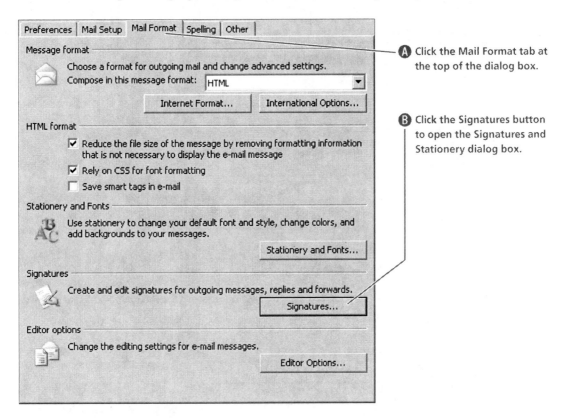

Ⓐ Click the Mail Format tab at the top of the dialog box.

Ⓑ Click the Signatures button to open the Signatures and Stationery dialog box.

3. Click the New button in the Signatures and Stationery dialog box.

4. Follow these steps to create a new signature:

Ⓐ Type **office** for the name of the signature and click OK.

Ⓑ Click in the signature box and then type the text shown here, tapping Enter twice after John Smith and tapping Enter once after all other lines.

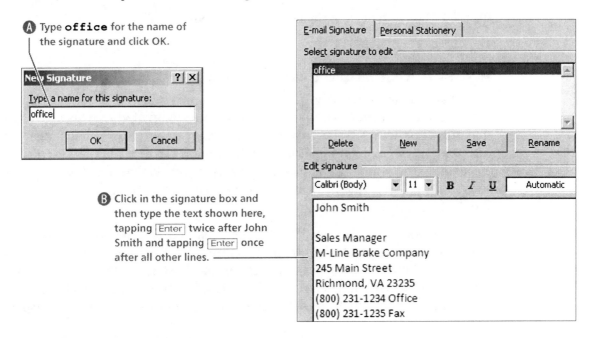

5. Click OK to return to the Mail Format page of the Options dialog box.

6. Click the Signatures button again to reopen the Signatures and Stationery dialog box.

7. Follow these steps to create an alternate signature:

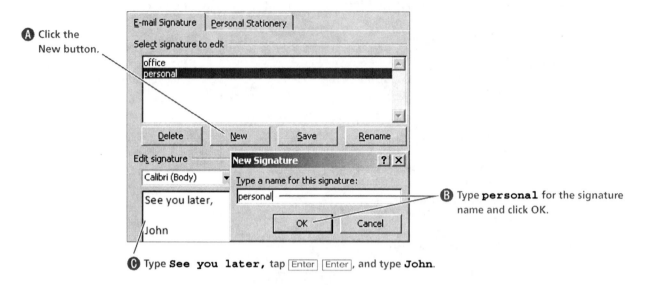

Ⓐ Click the New button.

Ⓑ Type **personal** for the signature name and click OK.

Ⓒ Type **See you later,** tap ⌷Enter⌷ ⌷Enter⌷, and type **John**.

8. Follow these steps to set the *office* signature as the default signature used for all new messages, replies, and forwards:

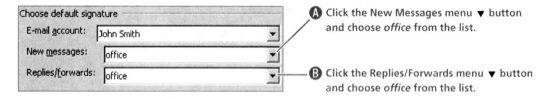

Ⓐ Click the New Messages menu ▼ button and choose *office* from the list.

Ⓑ Click the Replies/Forwards menu ▼ button and choose *office* from the list.

9. Change both the New Messages and Replies/Forwards options back to *(none)* and click OK.

10. Click OK again to close the Options dialog box.

Insert a Signature in a Message

Now that you have learned how to create a signature and how to set one up to be inserted automatically, you need to know how to insert one manually. Many people create multiple signatures but never set one up as a default. Many times, this is a good idea. For example, if you create a fun personal signature as a default but forget about it and send a letter to the president of the company, you would probably be very embarrassed when you realized what you did. Thus, sometimes it's better to forego having a signature inserted automatically and simply do it yourself.

When creating a new message, the Ribbon displays contextual tabs across the top. The Insert contextual tab contains buttons related to inserting something. For example, you can insert a file (which you will learn about at the end of this lesson), a picture, ClipArt, or a signature. Outlook stores all of the signatures you create and lets you pick and choose which to insert in any message. Use the Insert→Include→Signatures menu ▼ button to display the list of signatures.

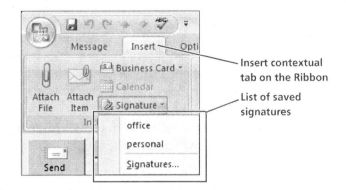

Insert contextual
tab on the Ribbon

List of saved
signatures

 ## Hands-On 2.5   Use the Ribbon to Insert a Signature

**On the
Web**
*If your computer does not have an email account set up, begin with step 1 below and perform the WebSim
online. Otherwise, skip step 1 and begin this exercise with step 2.*

1. Go to **labpub.com/learn/outlook07_fastcourse1** and click the link for
   Hands-On 2.5 Use the Ribbon to Insert a Signature.

2. Click the ⟨New⟩ button on the toolbar.

3. Follow these steps to complete the header portion of the message:

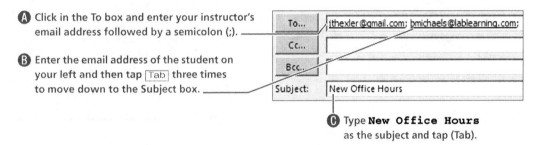

Ⓐ Click in the To box and enter your instructor's
email address followed by a semicolon (;).

Ⓑ Enter the email address of the student on
your left and then tap ⟨Tab⟩ three times
to move down to the Subject box.

Ⓒ Type **New Office Hours**
as the subject and tap (Tab).

4. Type the following message:

   **Due to spring-like conditions,
   effective immediately, the office
   will be closing at noon until
   further notice. Please plan
   accordingly.** ⟨Enter⟩

   ⟨Enter⟩

5. Choose Insert→Include→Signatures menu ▼
   button from the Ribbon.

6. Choose *office* from the list to insert John's business
   signature.

7. Click the ⟨Send⟩ button.

Attaching Files

Outlook allows you to attach any kind of file to an email message, including other Outlook items. John's position as the sales manager requires that he write many sales letters in Microsoft Word. In the past, he would print, fold and stuff the letters in envelopes, put stamps on the envelopes, and then head off to the post office. Now he's thrilled to find out how much time and money he will save by simply attaching the document to a message and sending the message to all of his distributors at once. Plus, he remembers from the Multiple Recipients section earlier in this lesson that if he uses the Bcc box to enter the email addresses, his customers will not see to whom he sent the same letter.

Either the Message tab or the Insert tab can be selected to access the Attach File command, which is listed under the Include command group on the Ribbon.

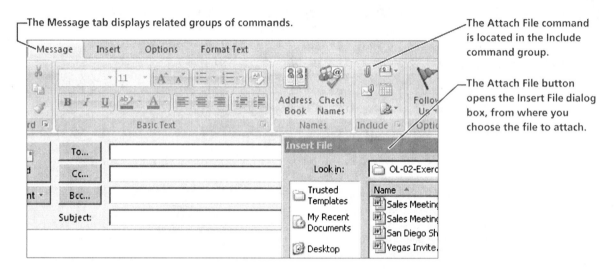

The Message tab displays related groups of commands.

The Attach File command is located in the Include command group.

The Attach File button opens the Insert File dialog box, from where you choose the file to attach.

After you attach a file, a new box appears under the Subject box and displays the attached file-name.

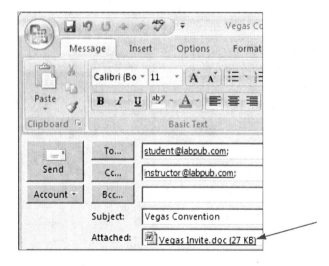

Hands-On 2.6   **Attach Files to Messages**

 If your computer does not have an email account set up, begin with step 1 below and perform the WebSim
On the Web *online. Otherwise, skip step 1 and begin this exercise with step 2.*

1. Go to **labpub.com/learn/outlook07_fastcourse1** and click the link for
    Hands-On 2.6: Attach Files to Messages.

2. Click the New button.

3. Address the message to the student on your left and carbon copy your instructor.

4. Type **Vegas Convention** as the subject.

5. Click in the message box and type the following: **I've attached the invitation.**

6. Choose Message→Include→Attach File button from the Ribbon.

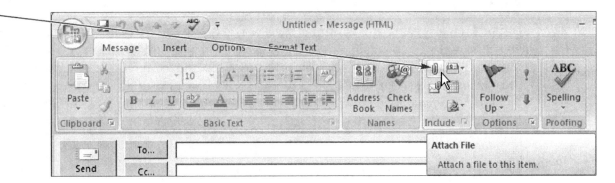

7. Follow these steps to insert a file:

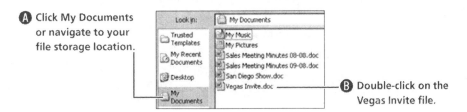

Ⓐ Click My Documents or navigate to your file storage location.

Ⓑ Double-click on the Vegas Invite file.

8. Send the message.

9. Click the New button.

10. Address the message to your instructor and the student to your right.

11. Type **San Diego Information** as the subject.

12. Type the following message:
    **Attached is the information we will be presenting at the San Diego
    show. I hope to see you at our booth.**

    John

13. Choose Message→Include→Attach File button from the Ribbon.

14. Navigate to My Documents or your file storage location.

15. Double-click on the San Diego Show file in the Insert file window.

16. Send the message.

17. Click the 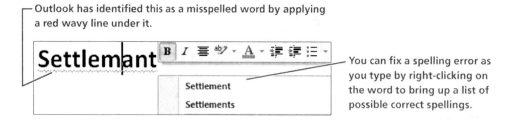 button and address the message to the student on your left, and carbon copy the instructor.

18. Type **Message with Attachment** as the subject.

19. Type the following in the message box: **Please review the attached file.**

20. Attach the Sales Meeting Minutes 09-08 file to the message.

21. Send the message.

Spell Check

Outlook has a spelling and grammar checker you can use to check for spelling errors in the body of a message, in an appointment, or in the Notes section of a contact. John will find this feature very useful, since he is a fairly new typist. He must still proofread the message, because the spelling checker will only mark a word as a possible error if it is not already in the Outlook dictionary. For example, he would probably be very embarrassed if a message went out about the results of the "Broad Meeting" instead of the "Board Meeting." You can see why proof-reading is so important!

Methods to Correct Spelling Errors

A possible spelling error is indicated with a red wavy line under the word. You can fix the problems as you type, or you can wait until you have completed the message and check for errors all at once by opening the Spelling dialog box.

You can correct a mistake by clicking the right mouse button and clicking the correct word in the options menu, or you can simply select the word and retype it.

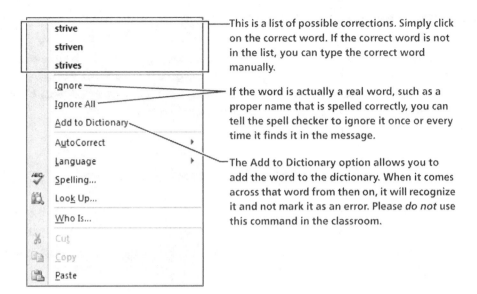

This is a list of possible corrections. Simply click on the correct word. If the correct word is not in the list, you can type the correct word manually.

If the word is actually a real word, such as a proper name that is spelled correctly, you can tell the spell checker to ignore it once or every time it finds it in the message.

The Add to Dictionary option allows you to add the word to the dictionary. When it comes across that word from then on, it will recognize it and not mark it as an error. Please *do not* use this command in the classroom.

The upper section of the Spelling dialog box displays the entire sentence containing the error, which is highlighted in red. The lower section displays a list of possible corrections.

The Not in Dictionary box displays the entire sentence and indicates the possible error in red. You can edit the highlighted word if the spelling check doesn't offer the correct suggestion.

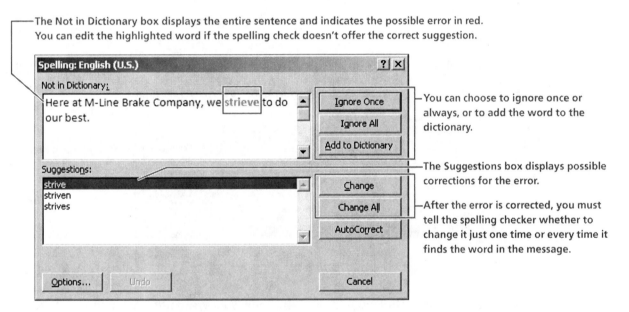

You can choose to ignore once or always, or to add the word to the dictionary.

The Suggestions box displays possible corrections for the error.

After the error is corrected, you must tell the spelling checker whether to change it just one time or every time it finds the word in the message.

 Hands-On 2.7   **Check the Spelling in a Message**

On the Web *If your computer does not have an email account set up, begin with step 1 below and perform the WebSim online. Otherwise, skip step 1 and begin this exercise with step 2.*

1. Go to **labpub.com/learn/outlook07_fastcourse1** and click the link for Hands-On 2.7: Check the Spelling in a Message.

2. Click the New button.

3. Address the message in the To box to the student on your left.

4. Type **Special Message** in the Subject box and then type the following message exactly as shown, including the typos:

Here at M-Line Brake Company, we strieve to do our best and I hope you will agree. Ferman Esco, Sales Manager at our affiliate, Belden Calipers, has agreed to a joint special ths month. I will send farther details in the next few days. ⌈Enter⌉

⌈Enter⌉

[Your Name]

5. Follow these steps to correct the first spelling error:

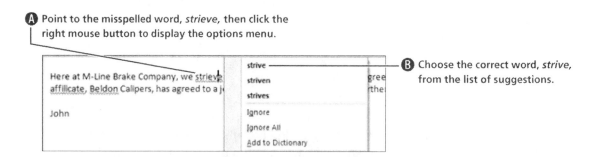

Ⓐ Point to the misspelled word, *strieve*, then click the right mouse button to display the options menu.

Ⓑ Choose the correct word, *strive*, from the list of suggestions.

6. Right-click on *Ferman,* which is the correct spelling, and choose Ignore from the options menu.

7. Choose Message→Proofing→Spelling and Grammar 🔲 button from the Ribbon.

8. Follow these steps to address the next error in the message:

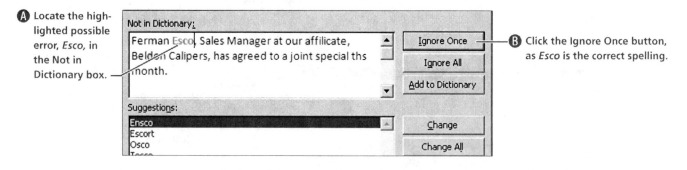

Ⓐ Locate the highlighted possible error, *Esco*, in the Not in Dictionary box.

Ⓑ Click the Ignore Once button, as *Esco* is the correct spelling.

9. Click the Change button to accept the suggested word *affiliate* for the next error.

10. Since none of the suggestions are the correct one, double-click the highlighted word *Beldon* in the Not in Dictionary section.

11. Type **Baldwin**, tap the ⌈Spacebar⌉, and click the Change button.

12. Click the Change button to accept the word *this* in the suggestion list.

13. Click OK in the spelling check is complete message box.

14. Proofread the last sentence of the message: *I will send farther details in the next few days*.

15. Double-click the word *farther* and type **further**.

16. Send the message.

Handling Incoming Messages

Outlook allows many choices of what to do with incoming messages. For example, you can read and delete, read and save, reply, forward, or print. If the message has a file attached to it, you can also save the attachment on your hard drive or other storage device, separate from the email message.

Send/Receive Button

When you click the [Send/Receive] button on the toolbar, Outlook first sends any messages still in the Outbox, and then checks the mail server for any new messages. You can check for new messages at any time using the Send/Receive button. Sending messages will be covered later in this lesson.

Outlook allows you to keep multiple email accounts organized in a group called All Accounts. Whichever method is chosen for checking messages, automatically or manually, Outlook checks all accounts and delivers them to the Inbox. While the accounts are being checked for new messages, a progress box may display on the screen, much like the one below. When the check is finished, the box closes on its own.

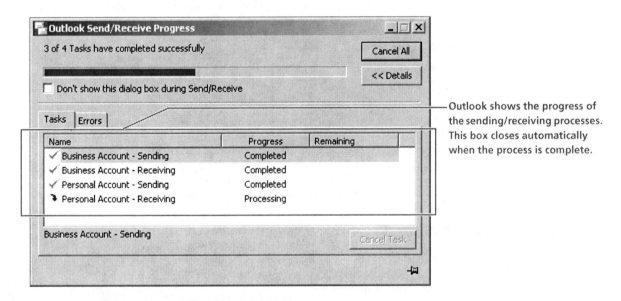

Outlook shows the progress of the sending/receiving processes. This box closes automatically when the process is complete.

Check Individual Accounts for Messages

There may be times that John wants to check for messages in only one account. In that case, he can use the Send/Receive menu ▼ button to choose which account to check.

When new messages arrive via either method, the following notification will occur:

- A short sound will play.

- A little icon of an unopened envelope will appear in the taskbar on the bottom, far-right corner of the screen. After you open the message, the envelope disappears from the taskbar.

 Hands-On 2.8   Check for Messages

 If your computer does not have an email account set up, begin with step 1 below and perform the WebSim online. Otherwise, skip step 1 and begin this exercise with step 2.

1. Go to **labpub.com/learn/outlook07_fastcourse1** and click the link for Hands-On 2.8 Check for Messages.

2. Click the [Send/Receive] button to check for messages in all accounts.

3. Follow these steps to check for messages in one specific account:

A Click the Send/Receive menu ▼ button on the toolbar.

B Choose the first individual account name in the list of accounts.

C Click the Inbox link to check for messages only in that account.

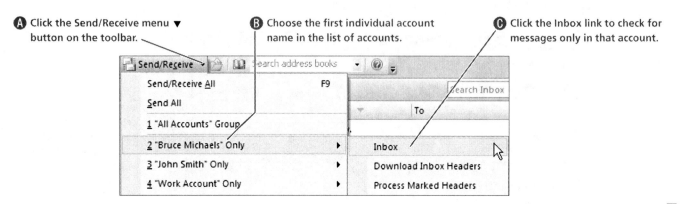

Read Messages

A new message is displayed first in the Inbox. The message is indicated as new with bold type and an unopened envelope icon. An attachment is indicated with a small paperclip. You can read the contents of the message in the Reading pane, or you can double-click on the message to open it in its own separate window. The

An unopened envelope and bold type indicates a new message that has not been read.

A paperclip indicates that a message contains an attachment.

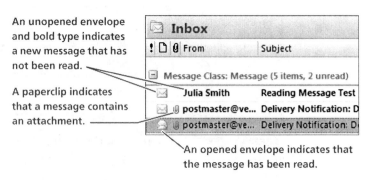

An opened envelope indicates that the message has been read.

latter method is helpful if the message is unusually long. It gives you a larger window in which to view the message, so you may not have to scroll down to read all of it.

Work with Attachments

When you receive a message with an attachment, you will notice the name of the file in the message box directly above the body of actual email message. Double-clicking on the attachment opens an option box, from which you choose whether to open and read the file or to save it. If you opt to open the file, you can still save it. The associated program opens automatically when you choose to *open* the attachment. A word of caution is important here. Viruses are passed often through email messages and their attachments, especially those with an extension of .exe. Be very mindful of the type of file and who it is from before you open it.

Hands-On 2.9   Read Messages

If your computer does not have an email account set up, begin with step 1 below and perform the WebSim online. Otherwise, skip step 1 and begin this exercise with step 2.

1. Go to **labpub.com/learn/outlook07_fastcourse1** and click the link for Hands-On 2.9 Read Messages.

2. Click the [⊞ Send/Receive] button to check for new messages.

3. Follow these steps to read a message:

Ⓐ Choose Special Message in the Subject column.

Ⓑ Read the message in the Reading pane.

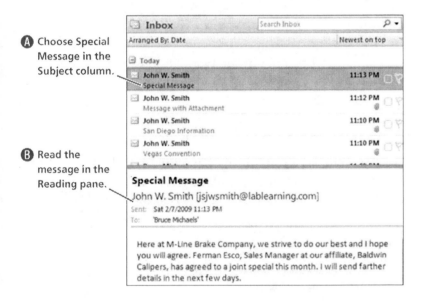

4. Follow these steps to read an attachment:

Ⓐ Choose Message with Attachment in the Inbox.

Ⓑ Double-click the attached file, Sales Meeting Minutes 09-08.doc.

Ⓒ Click Open in the Opening Mail Attachment box to open the Word document.

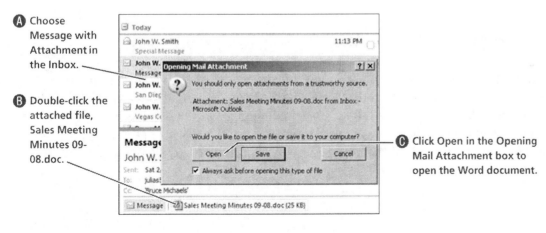

5. Click the Office 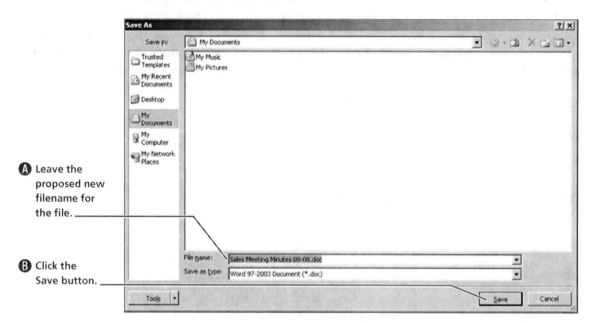 button in the upper-left corner of the Word window.

6. Click Save As in the menu.

7. Follow these steps to save the document in Microsoft Word in the My Documents folder:

A Leave the proposed new filename for the file.

B Click the Save button.

8. Click the Close ⊠ button in the upper-right corner of the Word window to close the document and Microsoft Word.

Respond to Messages

Outlook makes it easy for you to reply to a message and to share it with others by forwarding it (discussed below). When you reply, Outlook automatically places "RE:" at the beginning of the original subject. You may change the subject when replying or forwarding a message, if you wish.

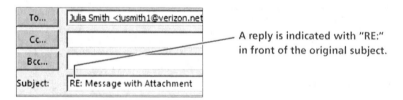

A reply is indicated with "RE:" in front of the original subject.

Reply or Reply to All

When you click the Reply button, Outlook opens a new window and places the sender's email address in the To box. This feature is extremely helpful, especially to a beginner like John, because it takes the worry out of making a mistake retyping the email address of the sender. Outlook also includes a copy of the sender's original message in the message box so it will be easy for the sender to see exactly what John is replying to. If you want to send your reply to everyone who originally received the message, you can simply use the Reply to All button instead of the Reply button.

Forward a Message

You may receive a message that wasn't intended for you or that you would like to share with others. You can do this with the Forward command. Like replying, Outlook opens a new window, but this time it leaves the To box empty so you can enter the email address to whom you would like to forward the message. When you forward a message, Outlook places "FW:" in front of the subject. This lets the recipients know without opening the message that it has been forwarded through you from someone else. And remember, when someone forwards you a file, you don't really know where it came from. Be careful when opening messages and attachments.

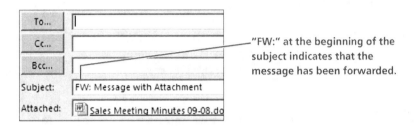

"FW:" at the beginning of the subject indicates that the message has been forwarded.

 ## Hands-On 2.10   Respond to Messages

 If your computer does not have an email account set up, begin with step 1 below and perform the WebSim online. Otherwise, skip step 1 and begin this exercise with step 2.

1. Go to **labpub.com/learn/outlook07_fastcourse1** and click the link for Hands-On 2.10 Respond to Messages.

2. Click Message with Attachment, if necessary.

3. Click the [Reply] button on the toolbar.

4. Type the following message:

   Thanks for including me. I am also forwarding your message to the person who was in my position before I started.

5. Send the message.

6. Choose Message with Attachment, if necessary.

7. Click the [Forward] button on the toolbar.

8. Follow these steps to forward the message:

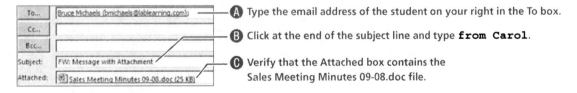

Ⓐ Type the email address of the student on your right in the To box.

Ⓑ Click at the end of the subject line and type **from Carol**.

Ⓒ Verify that the Attached box contains the Sales Meeting Minutes 09-08.doc file.

9. Click the [Send] button.

Print Messages

You can print a message just like you print any other document—and this is a feature that a beginner like John will surely appreciate. The default style to print messages is called Memo Style. It prints your name, the message header information (such as subject, date, etc.), and the actual message content. Use one of the following methods to print a message:

- The File→Print command opens the Print dialog box, from where you can choose certain options about printing your message.

- Clicking the Print button sends the message directly to the default printer without allowing you to set any print options.

Print button on the Outlook toolbar

To print an attachment, you can open it and print it from its particular program. For example, Microsoft Excel opens for an Excel spreadsheet attachment, Microsoft Word opens for a standard Word document, Adobe Acrobat opens for a PDF file attachment, and so forth. Or, if you are printing the email message it is attached to, you can use the Print dialog box and choose the option to also Print Attached Files.

 Hands-On 2.11   Print a Message and Its Attachment

On the Web *If your computer does not have an email account set up, begin with step 1 below and perform the WebSim online. Otherwise, skip step 1 and begin this exercise with step 2.*

1. Go to **labpub.com/learn/outlook07_fastcourse1** and click the link for Hands-On 2.11 Print a Message and Its Attachment.

2. Select Message with Attachment in the Inbox.

3. Choose File→Print from the menu bar.

4. Follow these steps to print the message with its attachment:

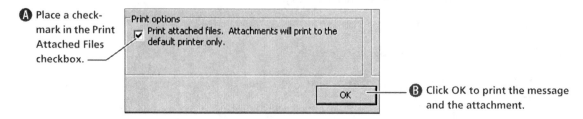

Ⓐ Place a checkmark in the Print Attached Files checkbox.

Ⓑ Click OK to print the message and the attachment.

Organizing Your Messages

You may want to keep some messages you send or receive for future reference. Leaving all incoming messages in the Inbox and outgoing messages in the Sent Items folder can become overwhelming as the number of messages grows. Typically, there are messages that somehow relate to each other. For example, John sends and receives messages to and from his distributors. An easy way for him to keep his messages organized might be to make a separate folder for each distributor. When he receives a message from a particular distributor, he can easily save the message in that folder.

Understand the Folder List

The folders in Outlook are arranged in a hierarchy where the top folder is always the Personal Folders. All other folders are contained inside this one. You can add a folder directly inside Personal Folders, or you can create a subfolder inside of another folder (for example, creating subfolders inside the Inbox to keep messages organized).

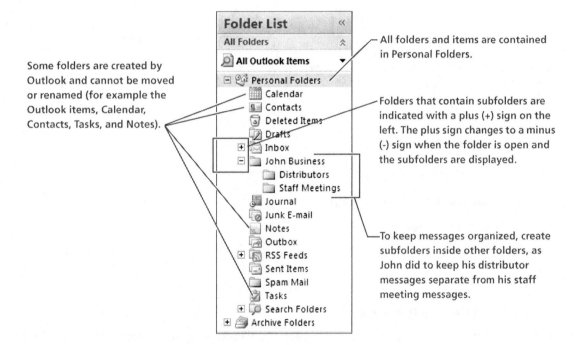

Some folders are created by Outlook and cannot be moved or renamed (for example the Outlook items, Calendar, Contacts, Tasks, and Notes).

All folders and items are contained in Personal Folders.

Folders that contain subfolders are indicated with a plus (+) sign on the left. The plus sign changes to a minus (-) sign when the folder is open and the subfolders are displayed.

To keep messages organized, create subfolders inside other folders, as John did to keep his distributor messages separate from his staff meeting messages.

Creating Folders

The folder structure you decide upon will be the one that works best for you. For example, maybe you don't deal with distributors like John does, but you do work on multiple projects. In that case, creating folders for each project name and saving messages related to each project may make more sense for you. You can create folders by right-clicking on the folder you want to put a folder inside of, or you can choose File→New→New Folder on the menu bar.

Hands-On 2.12 **Create a Folder**

1. Follow these steps to create a new folder inside Personal Folders:

Ⓐ Right-click on Personal Folders.

Ⓑ Click New Folder from the menu list.

2. Follow these steps to name the folder:

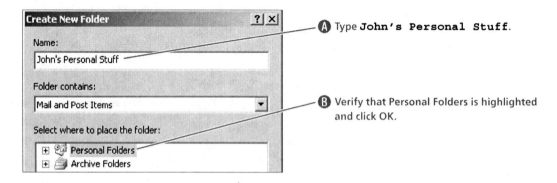

Ⓐ Type **John's Personal Stuff**.

Ⓑ Verify that Personal Folders is highlighted and click OK.

3. Click on Inbox in the folder list.

4. Click File→New ▼→Folder from the menu bar.

5. Type **John's Staff Meetings**.

6. Verify that Inbox is selected.

7. Click OK.

Move a Message to a Folder

Once you have folders created, you can move new incoming or outgoing messages into them. There are two methods to move a message to a folder:

■ Use Edit→Cut and Edit→Paste from the menu bar.

■ Drag the message over and onto the folder.

Whichever method you choose to move the message, you must highlight the folder that is receiving it. For example, when dragging a message from the Inbox, you simply let go of your mouse button once you have the desired folder highlighted. When using the cut and paste method, you must highlight the folder you wish to put the message in before you complete the paste. When you move a message that contains an attachment, the attached file moves right along with the message.

Move a Group of Messages

At times messages will fly back and forth: incoming, replying, forwarding, sending, and so forth. You may not take the time with each and every message right then to move it into a folder. No worry; you can select multiple messages and move them all at the same time from the Inbox or Sent Items folder into another one. To select multiple messages, hold down Ctrl and click individual messages in the list. Or, if you want to select the complete list, you can hold down Shift instead. In that case, you select the first message you want, hold down Shift and click on the last one in the list. The entire list is then highlighted and ready to move, or even delete, which you will learn about in the Delete Messages section.

 ## Hands-On 2.13 Move a Message

 If your computer does not have an email account set up, begin with step 1 below and perform the WebSim online. Otherwise, skip step 1 and begin this exercise with step 2.

1. Go to **labpub.com/learn/outlook07_fastcourse1** and click the link for Hands-On 2.13: Move a Message.

2. Click on Message with Attachment in the Inbox.

3. Choose Edit→Cut from the menu bar.

4. Choose John's Personal Stuff.

5. Choose Edit→Paste from the menu bar.

6. Follow these steps to move a group of messages:

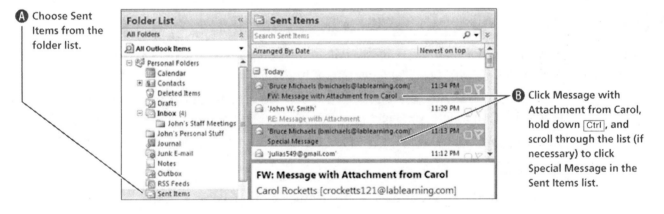

A Choose Sent Items from the folder list.

B Click Message with Attachment from Carol, hold down Ctrl, and scroll through the list (if necessary) to click Special Message in the Sent Items list.

7. Choose Edit→Cut from the menu bar.

8. Click the Inbox Plus Sign in the folder list, if necessary.

9. Choose John's Personal Stuff.

10. Choose Edit→Paste from the menu bar.

11. Follow these steps to drag a message to a folder:

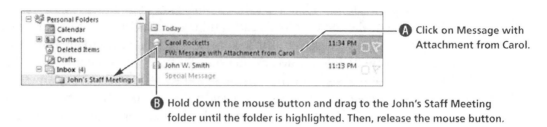

A Click on Message with Attachment from Carol.

B Hold down the mouse button and drag to the John's Staff Meeting folder until the folder is highlighted. Then, release the mouse button.

12. Click the John's Staff Meeting folder and verify that the message with its attachment was moved into the folder.

Delete Messages

When you delete a message from the Inbox or your Sent Items folders, it is sent to the Deleted Items folder. It is important to note that the message is still on your computer until you empty the Deleted Items folder. The nice thing about this is if you do delete a message by mistake, until the Deleted Items folder is emptied, you can move the message back into the folder from which you deleted it. If you are using Outlook in a corporate setting, your systems administrator probably has set up an automated system whereby your Deleted Items folder is emptied on a regular basis. You can empty the folder manually at any time using Tools→Empty Deleted Items Folder. Just like moving a group of messages at the same time, you can use the same procedure for selecting a group of messages to delete.

 Hands-On 2.14 **Delete Messages**

On the
Web *If your computer does not have an email account set up, begin with step 1 below and perform the WebSim online. Otherwise, skip step 1 and begin this exercise with step 2.*

1. Go to **labpub.com/learn/outlook07_fastcourse1** and click the link for Hands-On 2.14: Delete Messages.

2. Click Sent Items in the folder list.

3. Click the first message in the list.

4. Hold down the ⟨Shift⟩ key and click the last message you can see in the list.

5. Release ⟨Shift⟩ and tap ⟨Delete⟩ to move the messages to the Deleted Items folder.

6. Click on Deleted Items in the folder list.

7. Click Tools→Empty "Deleted Items" Folder.

8. Choose Yes in the message box that displays.

Archive Messages

All items in Outlook are stored in a Personal Folders (.pst) data file. As you accumulate more and more messages and other items such as calendars, the data file becomes especially large, which can ultimately slow down Outlook's performance. You can free up space by creating a separate .pst data file in the Archives Folder rather than storing everything in the Personal Folders. There may be messages that you do not need to keep in current folders but that you don't want to delete immediately. For example, you may

Archive folders already contain folders for the Outlook components.

Create your own folders in Archive Folders Inbox to keep your old messages organized.

have many messages related to an old project. It's possible that, in the future, you may need to refer to some information contained in those messages. Archive folders are available for the other Outlook components also. So, you could keep copies of your old calendars, for example.

You create folders in the Archive folder exactly the same way you create them in any other folder. You can move messages into the folders in Archive using the same methods as other folders. Another option is to set your own computer to archive automatically; however, understand that you do not have the control over where each item will be archived and, therefore, they will not be organized. Thus, if you think you'd like to keep some old messages handy just in case you need them, create your own archive folders in the Archive Folders Inbox and move messages into them accordingly.

 Hands-On 2.15   Create an Archive folder

1. Click the Archive Folders plus (+) sign in the folder list.

2. Right-click the Inbox under Archive Folders and choose New Folder.

3. Create a new folder named **Old meetings** and click OK.

4. Click the plus (+) sign next to Inbox under Archive Folders to view the new folder you created, if necessary.

Concepts Review

True/False Questions

1. Multiple signatures can be stored in Outlook.   (TRUE)   FALSE

2. Once you delete a file, it is gone completely from your computer.   TRUE   (FALSE)

3. Outlook can check for new messages at regular intervals automatically.   (TRUE)   FALSE

4. A signature can be inserted in messages automatically.   (TRUE)   FALSE

5. You can only send a message to one recipient at a time.   TRUE   (FALSE)

6. If you move a message that has a file attached to it, the attachment becomes unattached and gets lost.   TRUE   (FALSE)

7. To restrict multiple recipients so they can only see their own address, you can put the addresses in the Bcc box.   (TRUE)   FALSE

8. The spelling and grammar checker proofreads the message and reports all mistakes.   TRUE   (FALSE)

9. You can create a folder inside another folder.   (TRUE) FALSE

10. You can only reply to the original sender of a message.   TRUE   (FALSE)

Multiple Choice Questions

1. How does Outlook handle new email accounts?
   a. Outlook creates the email account.
   b. Outlook supplies you with an email account.
   c. Outlook does not provide email as an option.
   (d.) Outlook provides you with access to your email account.

2. Where do you find the Spelling button?
   a. On the Insert tab
   b. One the Outlook toolbar
   (c.) On the Message tab
   d. All of the above

3. How do you move a file into a folder?
   a. Choose Edit→Cut, choose the folder, and choose Edit→Paste.
   b. Drag the message from the Inbox and drop it onto a folder.
   (c.) Both A and B
   d. Neither A nor B

4. What type of file can you attach to an email message?
   a. A PDF file
   b. Another email message
   c. A piece of clip art
   (d.) All of the above

Working with Contact Information

In this lesson, you will learn about managing Outlook's Contacts list, the electronic equivalent of a rolodex that used to be found on every desk. Outlook provides you with an address book in which to store your contacts. Once you create them, you can always go back and edit or even delete contacts. Storing contacts in the Contacts list makes addressing messages much simpler than typing the addresses each time. And, the Contacts list can also be sorted in numerous ways. You can search for and choose one or more recipients from the Contacts list to go into the header section of a message. In this lesson, you will also learn how to save time addressing messages to the same people over and over again by creating distribution lists.

LESSON OBJECTIVES

After studying this lesson, you will be able to:

- Explore the Contacts views
- Work with contacts
- Use distribution lists

LESSON TIMING

- Concepts/Hands-On: 1 hr 15 min
- Concepts Review: 15 min
- Total: 1 hr 30 min

CASE STUDY: WORKING WITH CONTACTS

Alyssa Baker works for a training company and communicates with a variety of people. She's somewhat new to Outlook, but she's finding that it's pretty easy to learn. A colleague noticed that Alyssa was typing all of the email addresses into each message and suggested to her that she maintain her contacts in Outlook's address book, known as the Contacts list. He explained that when contacts are stored there, she can easily choose recipients for a message. Alyssa is excited about learning all the ways she can work with contacts in Outlook. She also realizes that she sends many messages to the same groups of people, and she wonders if there's a way to set up a standard list to send to rather than having to select the same names each time for each message. With a little research, she learns she can create a distribution list for those messages. Alyssa is anxious to see how easy it is to create, sort, and send messages to her contacts.

Additional learning resources are available at labpub.com/learn/outlook07_fastcourse1/

Managing Contact Information

Outlook offers several ways to display your list of contacts. You can maintain varied amounts of information about different contacts in Outlook's Contacts list. For example, you may only keep Aunt Helen's email address, while for a business client, you might want to store the company name, address, and phone/fax numbers. Contacts can be edited or deleted at any time using the Contacts window. You can delete a contact like you delete any other item: select it and tap Delete.

View the Contacts List

When Contacts is chosen in the Navigation pane, a list of available views is displayed. You can change the view by simply clicking on the view name. For example, you can view your contacts as a phone list, business cards, or address cards, to name a few. As your list of contacts grow, you can scroll through the list or use the Search Contacts box to find a particular contact. You will learn more about finding contacts a littler later in this lesson.

Clicking on one of these views displays the Contacts list in the center contents pane.

Here is a sample of a Contacts list in the Phone List view.

Search Contacts filters your contacts list after typing one or more characters of a contact name.

Hands-On 3.1   View Contacts

On the Web *If your computer does not have an email account set up, begin with step 1 below and perform the WebSim online. Otherwise, skip step 1 and begin this exercise with step 2.*

1. Go to **labpub.com/learn/outlook07_fastcourse1** and click the link for Hands-On 3.1: View Contacts.

2. Click Contacts in the Navigation pane, if necessary.

3. Click Address Cards in the view list.

4. Click Phone List view.

5. View the list. Click the contact for Donn Belker, if one exists, and tap Delete.

Working with Contacts

When you create a contact, Outlook stores it in the Contacts list. Alyssa will find it to be a time saver to address her messages by selecting her contacts from the Contacts list rather than typing them manually. The default format for storing the information is Last Name, First Name. This format is helpful because you then have an option to sort your list by either first or last name. You will learn more about sorting your contact later in this lesson.

Create a Contact in the Contacts Window

You can create a contact in the Contacts window and store as much information as you want about the person. The more information you put in, the more you will be able to see in the Contacts view, which can be quite helpful. For example, you may need to call someone but don't know their number. If you had entered their phone number in the contact's window, you could view the Contacts list and see the phone number right there in front of you.

Add the Sender of an Incoming Message to Contacts

Another method of adding a contact to the Contacts list is to right-click on the sender of an incoming message and choose Add Sender to Outlook Contacts. After you add it, a contact window opens automatically, giving you the opportunity to enter additional information, if you wish to do so.

 Hands-On 3.2   Create a New Contact

 If your computer does not have an email account set up, begin with step 1 below and perform the WebSim online. Otherwise, skip step 1 and begin this exercise with step 2.

1. Go to **labpub.com/learn/outlook07_fastcourse1** and click the link for Hands-On 3.2: Create a New Contact.

2. Follow these steps to open a contact window:

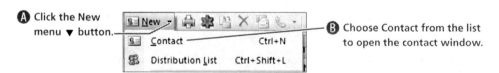

3. Follow these steps to add the imaginary contact as shown in the figure:

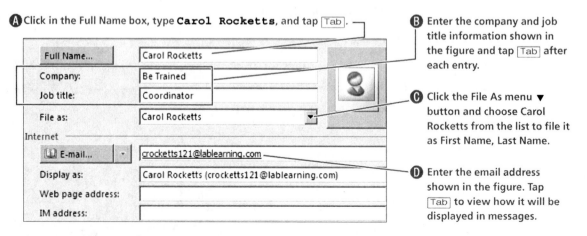

4. Follow these steps to enter the phone numbers and address for the contact:

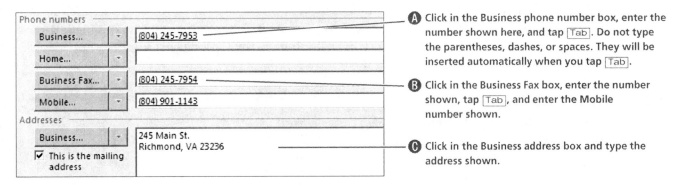

A Click in the Business phone number box, enter the number shown here, and tap `Tab`. Do not type the parentheses, dashes, or spaces. They will be inserted automatically when you tap `Tab`.

B Click in the Business Fax box, enter the number shown, tap `Tab`, and enter the Mobile number shown.

C Click in the Business address box and type the address shown.

5. Click in the Notes box and type following:
   Carol coordinates all classes, trainers, and equipment.

6. Click the Save & Close button.

7. Click Mail in the Navigation pane and click the John's Personal Stuff folder, and then follow these steps:

A Click Special Message in the Inbox.

B Right-click on the email address showing in the Reading Pane.

C Choose Add to Outlook Contacts from the menu list.

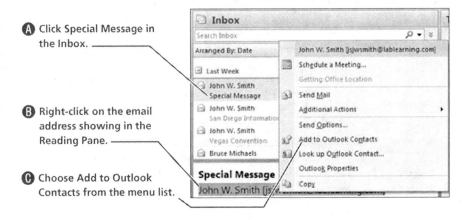

8. Click in the Company box and type **M-Line Brake Company**.

9. Click the File As menu ▼ button and choose John W. Smith from the list.

10. Click in the Business phone box and type **(804)562-1563**.
    (Remember, do not type the parentheses or the dash.)

11. Click the Save & New button.

12. Create two more contacts, one for your instructor and one named **Merle Humphrey** with the email address **merlehumphrey@gmail.com**.

Edit Contacts

To edit information, you must first find the desired contact and open the associated window. When the Navigation pane displays the views, a Search Contacts box appears in the upper-right corner of the contents pane. As you begin to type, the Contacts list filters contacts to display the name(s) that begin with those letters.

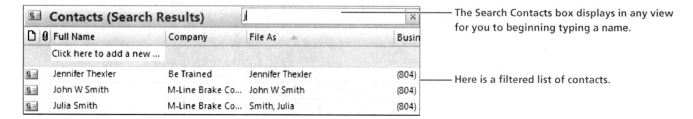

The Search Contacts box displays in any view for you to beginning typing a name.

Here is a filtered list of contacts.

 ### Hands-On 3.3   Edit a Contact

 If your computer does not have an email account set up, begin with step 1 below and perform the WebSim online. Otherwise, skip step 1 and begin this exercise with step 2.

1. Go to **labpub.com/learn/outlook07_fastcourse1** and click the link for Hands-On 3.3: Edit a Contact.

2. Follow these steps to find and edit the Merle Humphrey contact:

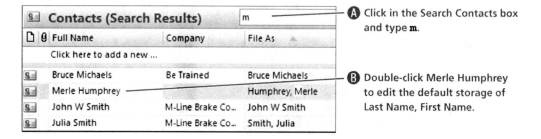

A Click in the Search Contacts box and type **m**.

B Double-click Merle Humphrey to edit the default storage of Last Name, First Name.

3. Click the File As menu ▼ button and choose the First Name, Last Name format.

4. Click in the Business address box and type **1701 Jump St**, tap ⌷Enter⌷, and type **Hanover, VA 23111**.

5. Click the Save & Close button.

Sort the Contacts List

By default, the Contacts list is sorted alphabetically by first name; however, you may wish to have it sorted differently. For example, if you deal with a variety of companies, you may wish to sort your list by company name. Or, if you have stored all your contacts by last name first, you may wish to sort by last name. There are column headers at the top of each column when you are viewing the list in Phone List view to use for sorting. The first click on a header sorts the list in ascending order and the second click changes the sort to descending order. When you change the sort order, it remains in that order until you change it again—even if you close and reopen Outlook.

Column headings in Phone List view

 Hands-On 3.4   Sort the Contacts List

 On the *Web* *If your computer does not have an email account set up, begin with step 1 below and perform the WebSim online. Otherwise, skip step 1 and begin this exercise with step 2.*

1. Go to **labpub.com/learn/outlook07_fastcourse1** and clickGo to labpub.com/learn/ outlook07_fastcourse1 and click the link for Hands-On 3.4: Sort the Contact List.

2. Click the File As column header to change the sort order from Full Name to the format in which it was stored.

3. Click the Company column header to sort the list by company name.

4. Click the Full Name header to change back to the original sort order.

Send Messages to Contacts

Once you have contacts entered in the Contacts list, it is easy to address messages. When you type email addresses, there is always the possibility of typing it incorrectly. In addition, as your list of contacts grows, it will become more difficult to remember all of them. After you open a new message window, you can click the To, Cc, or Bcc button to display a list of your contacts. If you want each recipient restricted to viewing only their own name, address the message in the Bcc box rather than the To box.

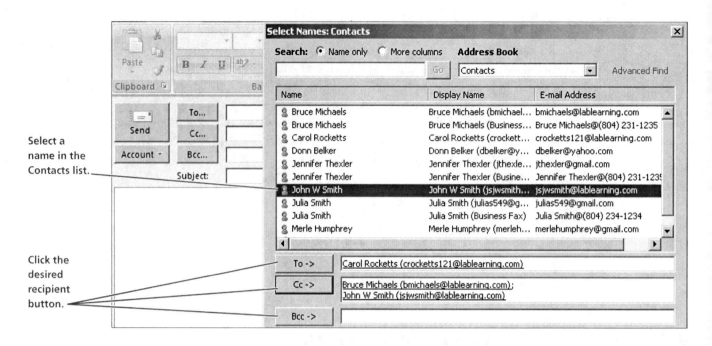

Select a name in the Contacts list.

Click the desired recipient button.

 Hands-On 3.5   Send a Message to a Contact

On the Web

If your computer does not have an email account set up, begin with step 1 below and perform the WebSim online. Otherwise, skip step 1 and begin this exercise with step 2.

1. Go to **labpub.com/learn/outlook07_fastcourse1** and click the link for Hands-On 3.5: Send a Message to a Contact.

2. Click Mail in the Navigation pane.

3. Click the ⬛New button to open a new message window.

4. Follow these steps to address the message using the address book:

Ⓐ Click the To button in the message header.

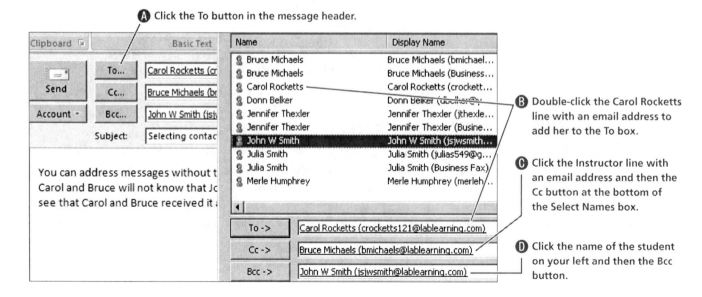

Ⓑ Double-click the Carol Rocketts line with an email address to add her to the To box.

Ⓒ Click the Instructor line with an email address and then the Cc button at the bottom of the Select Names box.

Ⓓ Click the name of the student on your left and then the Bcc button.

5. Click OK.

6. Type **Selecting contacts from the address book** in the Subject box and tap `Tab`.

7. Type the following in the message box:

   You can address messages without typing the addresses by using the contacts list in the address book. Carol and the instructor will not know that the student on your left also received the message because he is in the Bcc box. The student will see that Carol and the instructor received it also because they are in the To and Cc boxes.

8. Click the Send button.

Working with Distribution Lists

A quick way to send messages to the same group of people is to create a distribution list. This feature will definitely save Alyssa much time, since she sends messages quite often to groups of people. That is, some messages go to all instructors, while others are sent to all students. Once you create a distribution list, its name appears alphabetically in the Contacts list. When you want to send a message to the group of people in the list, you simply address the message to the distribution list name. The contacts you place in a distribution list will still appear in your complete list of contacts, so you can still send them individual messages.

Creating Distribution Lists

You create a distribution list in the Distribution List window. When you create a list, you give it a unique name and then add members to the list. You can also remove someone from a list. For example, if you created a distribution list for your managers and one gets promoted out of the department, you can remove that person and add his/her replacement to the list.

 Hands-On 3.6   Create a Distribution List

 If your computer does not have an email account set up, begin with step 1 below and perform the WebSim online. Otherwise, skip step 1 and begin this exercise with step 2.

1. Go to **labpub.com/learn/outlook07_fastcourse1** and click the link for Hands-On 3.6: Create a Distribution List.

2. Follow these steps to open a Distribution List window:

Ⓐ Click the New menu ▼ button.

Ⓑ Choose Distribution List.

3. Type **Students** in the Name box of the open Distribution List window.

4. Follow these steps to add members to the group:

Ⓐ Choose Distribution List→Members→Select Members from the Ribbon to open the window from which to choose the members.

Ⓑ Double-click on the names Carol Rocketts, the instructor, and Merle Humphrey in the Select Members: Contacts window to add their names to the Members box window.

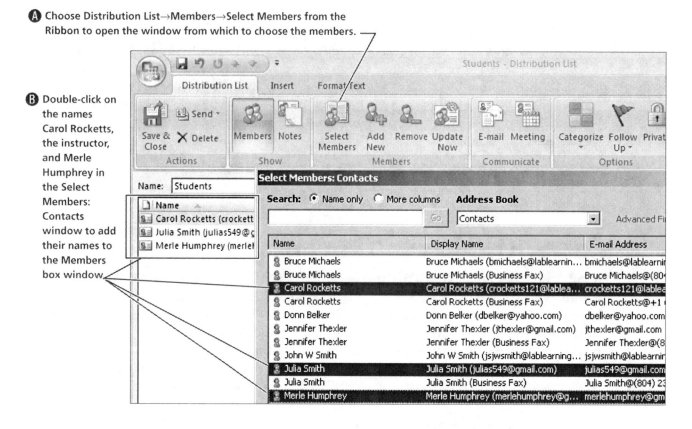

5. Click OK.

6. Click the Save & Close button.

Send Messages to Groups

When you create a distribution list, its name appears in the list of contacts in alphabetical order. A distribution list is denoted in the Contacts list by an icon with two people on it.

Individual contact name indicated with an icon of a business card with a face on it

Distribution list icon

To send a message to everyone in a distribution list, you start the message like any other message; but instead of addressing it to multiple recipients, you simply choose the distribution list name from the Contacts list.

If your computer does not have an email account set up, begin with step 1 below and perform the WebSim online. Otherwise, skip step 1 and begin this exercise with step 2.

1. Go to **labpub.com/learn/outlook07_fastcourse1** and click the link for Hands-On 3.7: Send a Message to a Group.

2. Click Mail in the Navigation pane.

3. Click the New button.

4. Click the To... button to display the list of contacts.

5. Follow these steps to send a message to a group:

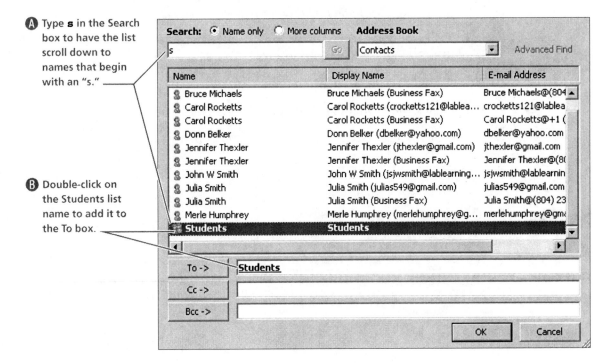

Ⓐ Type **s** in the Search box to have the list scroll down to names that begin with an "s."

Ⓑ Double-click on the Students list name to add it to the To box.

6. Click OK.

7. Follow these steps to complete the message:

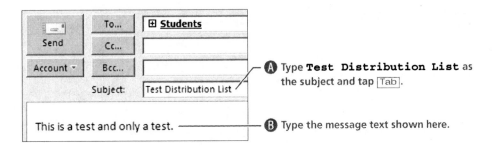

Ⓐ Type **Test Distribution List** as the subject and tap Tab.

Ⓑ Type the message text shown here.

8. Click the Send button.

Revise a Distribution List

You can remove a contact or edit information for a contact in a distribution list. When you edit information of someone in a list, it automatically updates the information for that person in the complete Contacts list. One important fact to point out is that when you open a distribution list to remove a contact, you must use the Remove command and not the Delete command. If you accidently use Delete, you are actually deleting the entire list—not just that one contact. You cannot undo the process in this case. You will have to re-create the distribution list.

 Hands-On 3.8   Edit a Distribution List

 If your computer does not have an email account set up, begin with step 1 below and perform the WebSim online. Otherwise, skip step 1 and begin this exercise with step 2.

1. Go to **labpub.com/learn/outlook07_fastcourse1** and click the link for Hands-On 3.8: Edit a Distribution List.

2. Click Contacts in the Navigation pane.

3. Double-click the Students list to open the distribution list window.

4. Follow these steps to remove a member from a list:

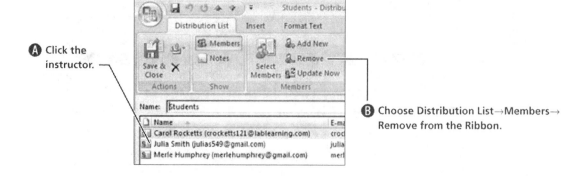

Ⓐ Click the instructor.

Ⓑ Choose Distribution List→Members→ Remove from the Ribbon.

5. Choose Distribution List→Members→Select Members from the Ribbon.

6. Double click on Merle Humphrey, click OK to replace the instructor in the distribution list, and click OK.

7. Click the Save & Close button.

Concepts Review

True/False Questions

1. All information is required to be filled in for each contact in the Contacts list. TRUE *FALSE*

2. When the Navigation pane is displaying the Contacts views, you can open a contact to edit information. *TRUE* FALSE

3. You can filter a contact list by typing in the Search Contacts box. *TRUE* FALSE

4. Contacts can only be filed by Last Name, First Name. TRUE *FALSE*

5. When you put a contact in a distribution list, the name disappears from the complete list of contacts. TRUE *FALSE*

6. You can sort the contacts list by First Name, Last Name or by Company Name. *TRUE* FALSE

7. Once someone is added to a distribution list, they cannot be removed from it. The distribution list must be deleted and re-created. TRUE *FALSE*

8. You can only put a distribution list name in the To box of a message. TRUE *FALSE*

9. If you accidentally delete a distribution list, you cannot undo the action. *TRUE* FALSE

10. To delete someone from a distribution list, select the name from the opened list and then tap Delete. TRUE *FALSE*

Multiple Choice Questions

1. Which of the following are ways you can view your contacts?
   a. Address cards
   b. Distribution lists
   c. Phone list
   d. Both A and C
   e. All of the above

2. How can you edit contact information?
   a. While viewing it in the Contents pane
   b. When opened in the Contacts window
   c. You cannot edit information for a contact
   d. Both A and B

3. What happens when you put a distribution list name in the Bcc box of a message?
   a. All recipients can see everyone it was sent to.
   b. Each recipient can only see their own address.
   c. Nothing appears in the Bcc box.
   d. None of the above

4. What happens when you edit information of someone in a distribution list?
   a. The information is only updated in the distribution list.
   b. You cannot edit information of a contact in a distribution list.
   c. The information in the complete Contacts list is automatically updated.
   d. All information is deleted.

LESSON 4

Using the Calendar

In this lesson, you will learn how to use several Calendar features. Calendars are used to schedule time for appointments and meetings. Depending on your needs, you can view your calendar in one of three views: Day, Week, or Month. You can also schedule appointments that happen on a regular basis (recurring appointments). You will also learn about reminders, which are set to remind you of upcoming events. Finally, in this lesson, you will learn how to share your calendar while keeping certain items private only to you.

LESSON OBJECTIVES

After studying this lesson, you will be able to:

- Create and edit appointments and meetings
- Set recurring appointments
- Explore Calendar views
- Share your calendar
- Print a calendar

LESSON TIMING

- Concepts/Hands-On: 2 hrs 15 min
- Concepts Review: 15 min
- Total: 2 hrs 30 min

CASE STUDY: WORK WITH CALENDARS

Stefanie Bentley is an event planner who must manage her time wisely. She knows that event planning is all about organization: where to be at what time, who she's meeting, for what purpose, and so forth. Outlook's Calendar feature is the perfect place to keep Stef organized. When she sets up appointments, she can also set reminders to pop up. When Stef starts out in the morning, she will display her calendar to see what's in store for her that day. If she needs to make appointments for later in the week, she can view her schedule for the entire week so she doesn't set conflicting appointments. Stef wants to have a hard copy of her calendar to carry with her, and she wants to share her calendar with her assistant. She can do both with Outlook, plus she can still keep certain items on her calendar private.

Working with Appointments

You create appointments for whenever you need time blocked out of your day. For example, you may have a doctor's appointment, a meeting with a client, or need scheduled time to work on a task that you create. You will learn about creating tasks in Lesson 5, Using Notes, Tasks, and the Journal. You must open an Appointment window to edit any information in it, such as the duration, to set a reminder, to add extra notes, and so on. You can invite attendees to meetings also, which you will learn about in the next section.

Schedule an Appointment

 When you choose the Calendar button in the Navigation pane, the calendar opens in Day view, displaying times in one-half hour increments. After the calendar opens, you can double-click at the desired starting time of your appointment. The calendar displays the title of an appointment and the shaded area indicates the duration. When you have an all-day conference, you can mark a checkbox that this is an all day event.

Hands-On 4.1   Create a New Appointment

1. Click the Calendar 🗓 button on the Navigation pane.

2. Follow these steps to create an appointment for next week:

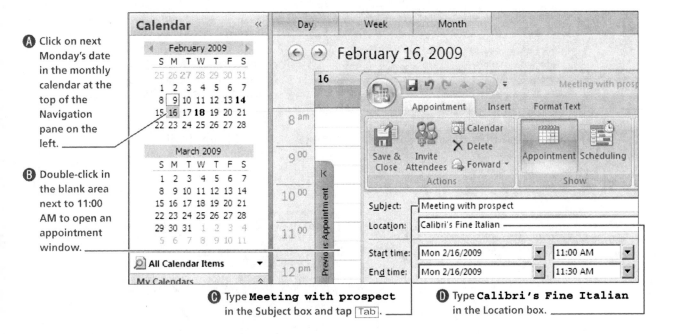

Ⓐ Click on next Monday's date in the monthly calendar at the top of the Navigation pane on the left.

Ⓑ Double-click in the blank area next to 11:00 AM to open an appointment window.

Ⓒ Type **Meeting with prospect** in the Subject box and tap [Tab].

Ⓓ Type **Calibri's Fine Italian** in the Location box.

3. Choose Appointment→Actions→Save & Close from the Ribbon.

Edit Appointments

You can edit any sections of an appointment when you open the appointment window. For example, you change the dates and times, set a reminder, or even enter special notes for yourself.

Change the Appointment Time or Date

Sometimes plans change, and appointments get postponed all the time. When you change the time in the appointment window, it moves the appointment to the new timeslot on the calendar view. Or, it's very quick and easy to move an appointment by dragging it. Moving an appointment to another day in the same week is easily done in Week view. You will learn more about views later in this lesson.

 Hands-On 4.2   Edit an Appointment

1. Double-click to open the Meeting with Prospect appointment.

2. Follow these steps to edit the appointment:

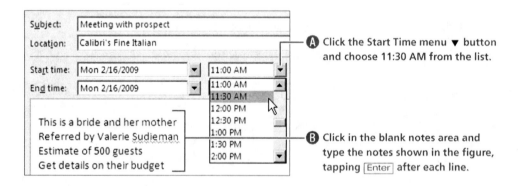

3. Click the End Time menu ▼ button and choose 1:30 PM from the list, and then click Save & Close .

4. Follow these steps to move an appointment:

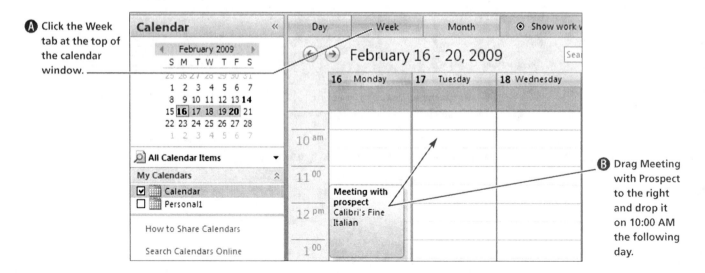

5. Drag the meeting back to 11:30 AM the previous day.

6. View the calendar to confirm that the appointment moved down to 11:30 AM and that the shaded box indicates that the meeting has expanded down to the end time of 1:30 PM.

Set a Reminder for an Appointment

You can set a reminder to pop up on the screen, prompting you of the upcoming appointment. A reminder can be set from five minutes up to two weeks prior to the appointment. Setting reminders will surely be an advantage for Stef, who has too many appointments to remember all on her own.

 Hands-On 4.3   Set a Reminder

1. Double-click the Meeting with Prospect appointment, then follow these steps to set a reminder for it:

Ⓐ Choose Appointment→Options→Reminder ▼ from the Ribbon.

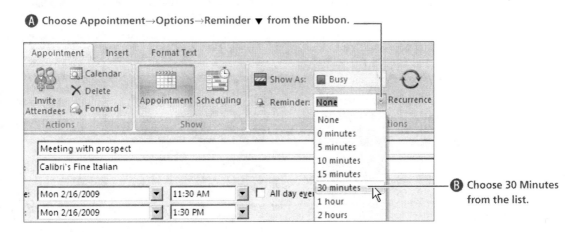

Ⓑ Choose 30 Minutes from the list.

2. Click the Save & Close button.

Invite Attendees

When you place an appointment on your calendar, it affects only your schedule; however, you can invite others to attend as well. At that point, the appointment is called a meeting, and you will notice this in the title bar of the open window. Attendees receive an invitation via email and have the option to accept or decline. If they choose to accept, the appointment is placed on their calendar and you receive notification that they will be attending. If they decline, the appointment is not placed on their calendar and they can opt to notify you that they have declined.

Hands-On 4.4   Invite Attendees to a Meeting

 If your computer does not have an email account set up, begin with step 1 below and perform the WebSim online. Otherwise, skip step 1 and begin this exercise with step 2.

1. Go to **labpub.com/learn/outlook07_fastcourse1** and click the link for Hands-On 4.4: Invite Attendees to a Meeting.

2. Double-click to open the Meeting with Prospect appointment on your calendar for next Monday.

3. Choose Appointment→Actions→Invite Attendees from the Ribbon.

4. Click the To... button, then double-click on the email addresses of the student on your left and your right, and your instructor.

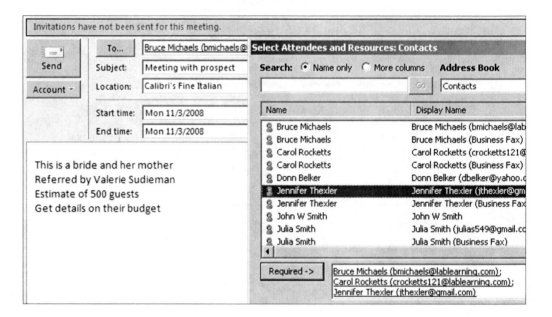

5. Click OK.

6. Follow these steps to view the changes to the Ribbon and to send the invitation:

Ⓐ Notice that the Appointment tab has become the Meeting tab.

Ⓑ View the absence of the Invite Attendees button; it's been replaced by the Cancel Invitation button.

Ⓒ Click the Send button.

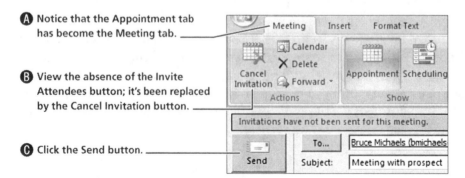

7. Click Mail in the Navigation pane.

8. Click the [Send/Receive] button if the Meeting Request has not arrived yet.

9. Follow these steps to accept the invitation:

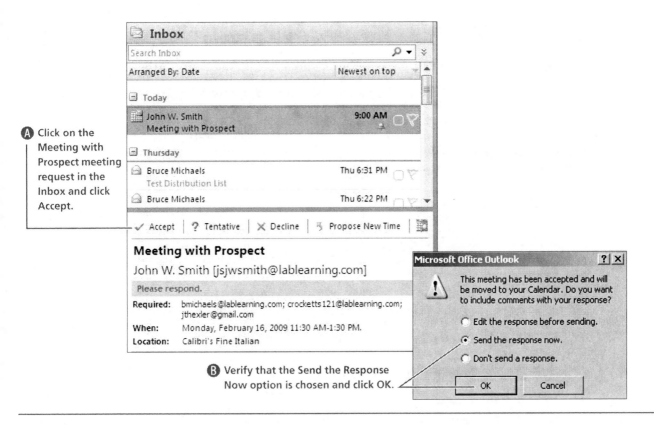

A Click on the Meeting with Prospect meeting request in the Inbox and click Accept.

B Verify that the Send the Response Now option is chosen and click OK.

Recurring Appointments

Recurring appointments are those that occur the same day and time each week, bi-monthly, monthly, and so forth. For example, you may have a weekly staff meeting on Monday's at 10:00 AM. Since Stef is in the event planning business, she does attend regular networking meetings to drum up more business. With her busy schedule, she will make good use of the recurring appointments feature.

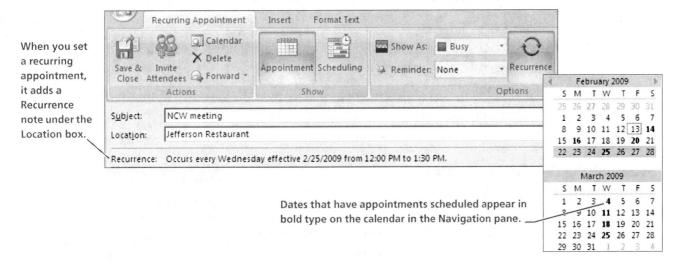

When you set a recurring appointment, it adds a Recurrence note under the Location box.

Dates that have appointments scheduled appear in bold type on the calendar in the Navigation pane.

1. Click on next Wednesday's date on the calendar in the Navigation pane.

2. Double-click on 12:00 PM to open an appointment window.

3. Follow these steps to begin creating the appointment:

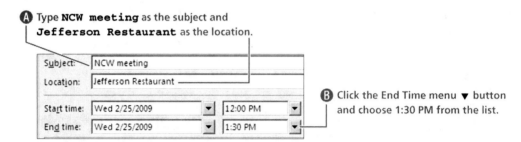

Ⓐ Type **NCW meeting** as the subject and **Jefferson Restaurant** as the location.

Ⓑ Click the End Time menu ▼ button and choose 1:30 PM from the list.

4. Choose Appointment→Options→Recurrence from the Ribbon.

5. Follow these steps to make the appointment a recurring event:

Ⓐ Click the button next to Monthly in the Recurrence Pattern section.

Ⓑ Click the button next to the day of the week option.

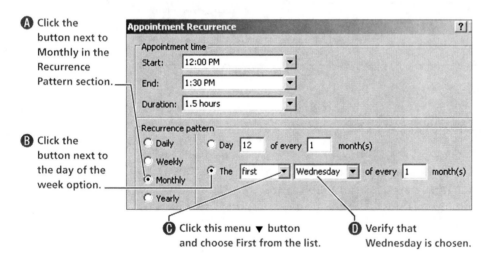

Ⓒ Click this menu ▼ button and choose First from the list.

Ⓓ Verify that Wednesday is chosen.

6. Click OK.

7. Click the Save & Close button.

8. Click the first Wednesday of the following month on the calendar in the Navigation pane to view the recurrence.

Editing Recurring Appointments

You can edit a recurring appointment by altering just one occurrence or the entire series. When you opt to change the entire series, whatever editing you perform affects every instance of that appointment. It is

Choose to edit individual occurrences or all occurrences.

important to note, however, that any exceptions made for an individual occurrence will be lost when you make a change to the entire series. For example, if you change a reminder for just one occurrence, but then edit the entire series to occur from weekly to monthly, the individual exception for the one reminder will be lost.

Delete a Recurring Appointment

Likewise, when you delete a recurring appointment, you have the option of deleting only one occurrence or the entire series. For example, let's say that you set up a monthly recurring appointment for the next year but then realize you will not be available in June or December. You can delete only those two occurrences. Once you delete an occurrence, it cannot be undone.

 Hands-On 4.6   Edit a Recurring Appointment

1. Double-click the NCW Meeting appointment on the calendar to open the Recurring Appointment window and then follow these steps:

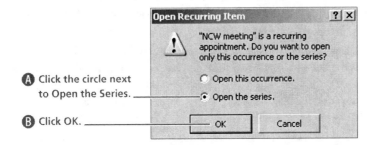

Ⓐ Click the circle next to Open the Series.

Ⓑ Click OK.

2. Choose Appointment→Options→Recurrence from the Ribbon.

3. Follow these steps to change the appointment time and recurrence:

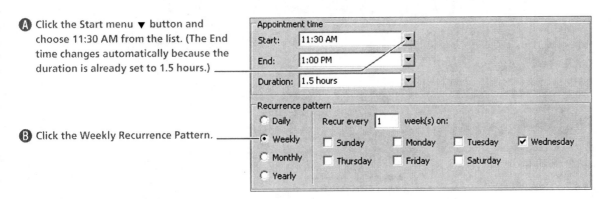

Ⓐ Click the Start menu ▼ button and choose 11:30 AM from the list. (The End time changes automatically because the duration is already set to 1.5 hours.)

Ⓑ Click the Weekly Recurrence Pattern.

4. Click OK.

5. Click OK again if a box appears to warn you that any exceptions will be lost because you are making changes to the entire series.

6. Click Save & Close.

7. Click on the last Wednesday of the following month in the Navigation pane.

8. Right-click the NCW Meeting appointment and then click Delete from the menu list.

9. Follow these steps to delete an individual occurrence of an appointment:

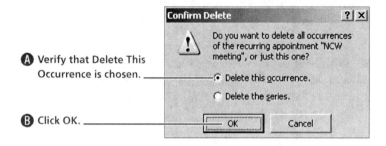

Ⓐ Verify that Delete This Occurrence is chosen.

Ⓑ Click OK.

Exploring the Calendar

The calendar displays your schedule in three different views: Day, Week, and Month. The type of schedule you maintain will determine which view works best for you. For example, you can use the Week view if you need visible details about each appointment this week, or you can use the Month view if you need only to see what dates do not currently have anything scheduled. Day and Week views also display your daily tasks at the bottom of the calendar. You can also share your calendar with others. You will learn about sharing later in this lesson.

No matter what view you are in on your calendar, you can easily get back to the current date using the Today button.

Calendar views include Day, Week, and Month.

The Monthly calendar in the Navigation pane allows you to jump quickly to a certain date.

The Back and Forward buttons allow you to move forward or back one day, week, or month depending on the selected view.

Details of events appear on the calendar in any view.

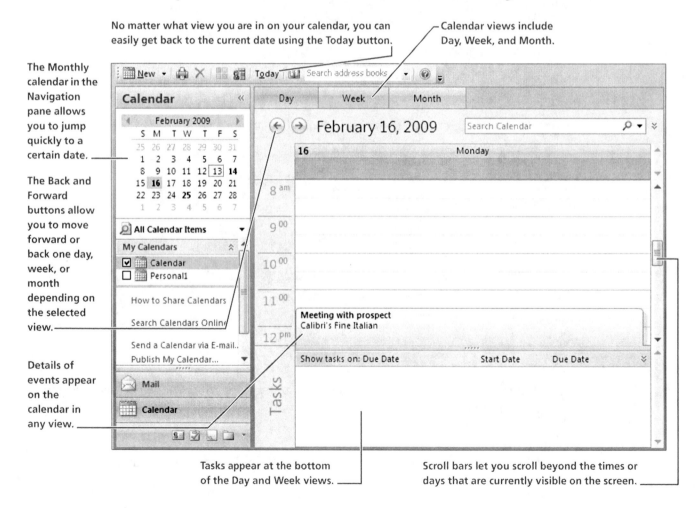

Tasks appear at the bottom of the Day and Week views.

Scroll bars let you scroll beyond the times or days that are currently visible on the screen.

Day View

Day view displays all events on the calendar for the chosen day. The scroll bars are used to navigate the times of the day. You can change the beginning and end default time options. The Forward and Back arrow buttons display the next or previous day's calendar. You will learn about changing options later in this lesson. Day view also displays daily tasks at the bottom of the calendar.

The Forward and Back arrow buttons scroll to other days one day at a time.

The default day begins at 8:00 AM and ends at 5:00 PM, and is shown in half-hour increments.

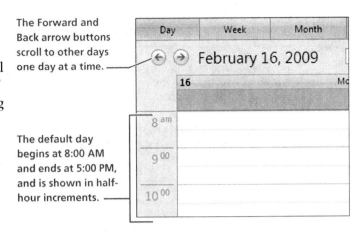

Week View

Week view is perfect when you want to check to see if you have any time for an appointment in the current week. You can show it as a Work Week or a Full Week.

Week view displays the week's date span.

The Forward and Back arrow buttons scroll through the calendar by weeks.

Options are available to display the Work Week or the Full Week.

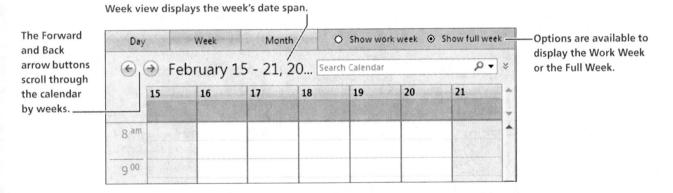

Month View

The Month view displays the entire month of events. Month view is handy when you want a quick look at what dates already have something scheduled and what dates you are free. You have three options of how much detail to display: Low hides all appointments, Medium displays a horizontal line in a date where something is scheduled, and High displays the appointment titles.

The Forward and Back arrow buttons scroll through the calendar one month at a time.

Choose what level of detail to display on the calendar.

Weekly timeframes are displayed down the left side of the monthly view.

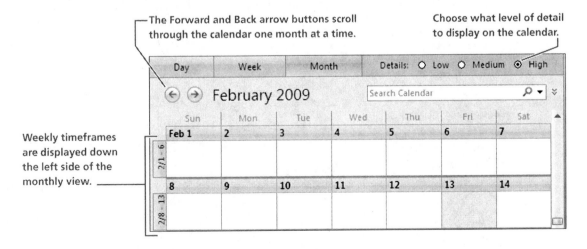

1. Click the Day tab at the top of the Calendar window.

2. Follow these steps to use the Day view:

Ⓐ Click the monthly calendar in the Navigation pane on the the date of the Meeting with Prospect meeting.

Ⓑ Click the Back ⊙ button to move back to one day.

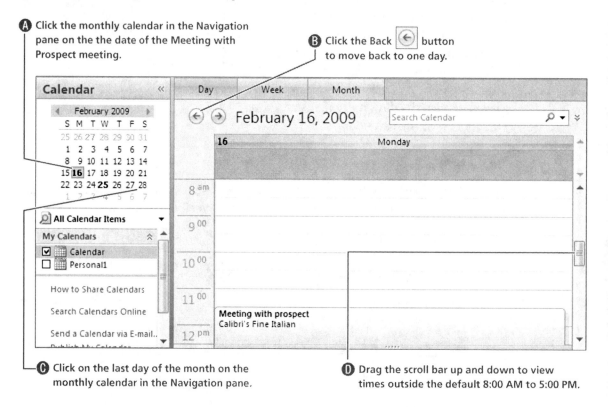

Ⓒ Click on the last day of the month on the monthly calendar in the Navigation pane.

Ⓓ Drag the scroll bar up and down to view times outside the default 8:00 AM to 5:00 PM.

3. Click the Meeting with Prospect date in the Navigation pane.

4. Follow these steps to view your calendar in Week view:

Ⓐ Click the Week view tab.

Ⓑ Click the Forward ⊙ button and watch the weekly dates change.

Then, click the Back ⊙ button to return to the previous week's calendar.

Ⓒ Verify that Show Work Week is chosen.

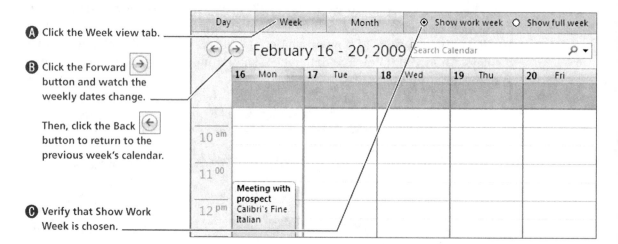

5. Follow these steps to navigate in Month view:

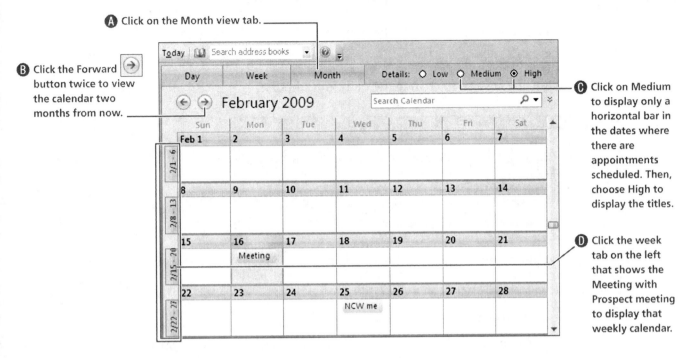

A Click on the Month view tab.

B Click the Forward button twice to view the calendar two months from now.

C Click on Medium to display only a horizontal bar in the dates where there are appointments scheduled. Then, choose High to display the titles.

D Click the week tab on the left that shows the Meeting with Prospect meeting to display that weekly calendar.

6. Click on the Day view tab.

Change Calendar Options

Certain options for calendars can be changed using Tools→Options on the menu bar. For example, you can change the reminder increments from the default of fifteen minutes. One of the most popular options to change is the daily work times, since gone are the days of everyone working the same shift of Monday through Friday, 8:00 AM to 5:00 PM. You can change these options to fit your schedule.

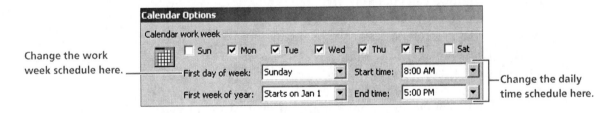

Change the work week schedule here.

Change the daily time schedule here.

1. Choose Tools→Options from the menu bar.

2. Click Calendar Options in the Options dialog box.

3. Follow these steps to change the daily work hours:

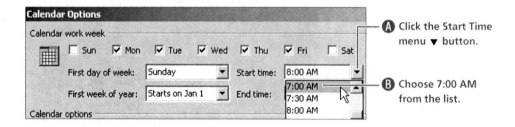

Ⓐ Click the Start Time menu ▼ button.

Ⓑ Choose 7:00 AM from the list.

4. Click the End Time menu ▼ button and choose 4:00 PM from the list.

5. Click OK to close the Calendar Options dialog box.

6. Click OK to close the Options dialog box.

7. Click Mail in the Navigation pane to leave Calendar view momentarily so you can return to see the results of changing the timeframe.

8. Click the Calendar ▦ button to verify that the calendar now displays the timeframe of 7:00 AM to 4:00 PM.

Sharing Calendars

There are many ways to share a calendar and this short course covers one way—sending a calendar via email. Those calendar items you marked as private can be shared or not. It's entirely up to you. The default option is set to not share them. When someone receives a calendar with items marked private, all they will see on your calendar is "Private Appointment" to indicate that you are not available at that time. The sharing options will vary in the Navigation pane depending on your Outlook configuration.

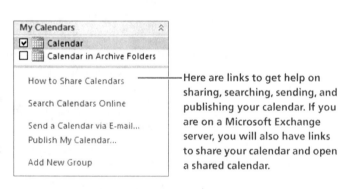

Here are links to get help on sharing, searching, sending, and publishing your calendar. If you are on a Microsoft Exchange server, you will also have links to share your calendar and open a shared calendar.

Custom Calendars

There may be special circumstances where you would like to have a separate calendar. If, for example, you are working on a team project, it may be beneficial to have a special calendar to share with the project team members. You create additional calendars using the File→New command, just like you do for creating a new folder, which you learned back in Lesson 2, Working with Email.

You can check or uncheck the calendars you want displayed.

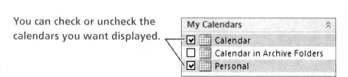

If you choose to share your default calendar, you can choose to keep certain items private. When you have multiple calendars, the Navigation pane displays them in a list under My Calendars.

Display Calendars

Multiple calendars are initially displayed side by side in the Calendar pane. When you want to check for conflicts between the two calendars, it may be easier to see if you overlay the calendars. For example, if your project team members send you their calendars, you can overlay them to watch for conflicts and determine if something needs to be changed. Outlook assigns calendar tabs different colors so you can easily tell them apart. When in Overlay mode, the calendar that is on the top can be edited. To change the order of calendars, simply click on the calendar name tab at the top of the window to put the desired one on top. You can tell which items are on the bottom calendar because their titles are partially shaded (the ones on the top calendar are in bold type).

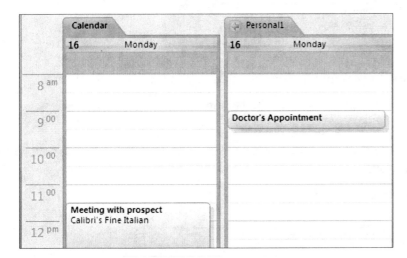

The default calendar and the new Personal calendar are color coded and displayed side by side in this illustration.

Here the calendars are displayed in Overlay mode with Personal on top. To put the default calendar on top, click its tab.

Copy Calendar Items

You can copy items from one calendar to another. The simplest way is to view the calendars side by side and drag the event over and onto the same time on the other calendar.

Mark Items as Private

Any item you have on your calendar, including appointments and meetings, can be marked as private. Later, if you decide to share your calendar with someone, there is an option to choose whether or not to share those items. A private item is identified with a padlock icon on the right of the event title.

1. Click Calendar in the Navigation pane, if necessary.

2. Click File→New→Calendar from the menu bar.

3. Follow these steps to create a new calendar:

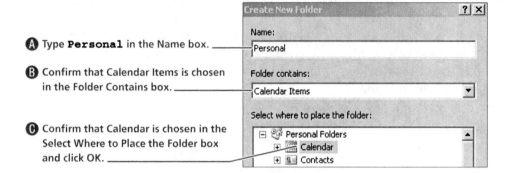

Ⓐ Type **Personal** in the Name box.

Ⓑ Confirm that Calendar Items is chosen in the Folder Contains box.

Ⓒ Confirm that Calendar is chosen in the Select Where to Place the Folder box and click OK.

4. Click the checkbox next to Personal under My Calendars in the Navigation Pane.

5. Click on an available time next Monday in the Personal calendar, type **Doctor's Appointment**, and tap Enter.

6. Click on another available time next Monday in the Personal calendar, type **Meet with supervisor**, and tap Enter.

7. Follow these steps to mark the item as private:

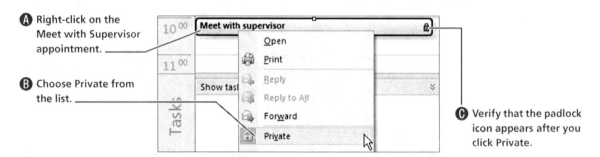

Ⓐ Right-click on the Meet with Supervisor appointment.

Ⓑ Choose Private from the list.

Ⓒ Verify that the padlock icon appears after you click Private.

8. Follow these steps to display the calendars in Overlay mode:

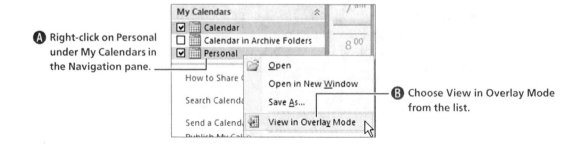

Ⓐ Right-click on Personal under My Calendars in the Navigation pane.

Ⓑ Choose View in Overlay Mode from the list.

9. Follow these steps to put the default calendar on top of the Personal calendar:

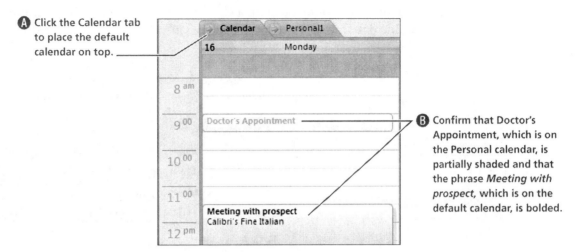

A Click the Calendar tab to place the default calendar on top.

B Confirm that Doctor's Appointment, which is on the Personal calendar, is partially shaded and that the phrase *Meeting with prospect*, which is on the default calendar, is bolded.

10. Right-click on the Personal calendar in the Navigation pane and choose View in Side-by-Side Mode.

11. Follow these steps to copy the Doctor's Appointment from the Personal calendar to the default calendar:

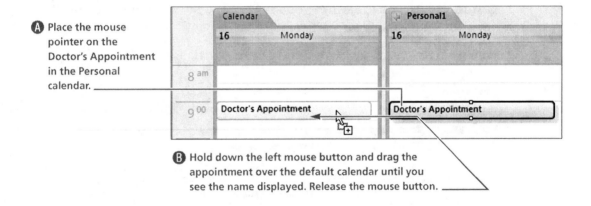

A Place the mouse pointer on the Doctor's Appointment in the Personal calendar.

B Hold down the left mouse button and drag the appointment over the default calendar until you see the name displayed. Release the mouse button.

12. Click the checkmark next to the default calendar in the Navigation pane to remove it so that only the Personal calendar is displayed.

Share Your Calendar through Email

A Calendar Snapshot is a picture of any of your calendars that you send via email to another person. Calendar Snapshots are not updated for the recipients when you make a change; thus, if you want your recipients to have the latest data, you will need to resend the calendar. The recipient can opt to view the calendar directly in the email message or open it as an Outlook calendar. They can then position your calendar side by side theirs or in Overlay mode.

Sending Options

You can set several options when you send a calendar to someone, such as sending the whole calendar or a specific date range. You can also specify if you want your private items included and what layout to send it in.

Choose the Date Range of the calendar to send.

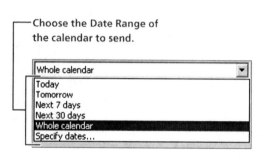

Advanced options offer the choice of whether to include private items and items with attachments.

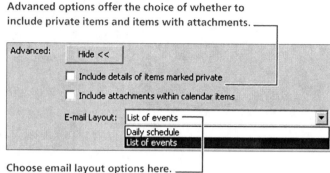

Choose email layout options here.

 ## Hands-On 4.10   Send a Calendar via Email

On the Web *If your computer does not have an email account set up, begin with step 1 below and perform the WebSim online. Otherwise, skip step 1 and begin this exercise with step 2.*

1. Go to **labpub.com/learn/outlook07_fastcourse1** and click the link for Hands-On 4.10: Send a Calendar via Email.

2. Follow these steps to open the Send a Calendar via E-mail dialog box:

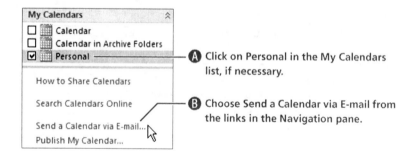

Ⓐ Click on Personal in the My Calendars list, if necessary.

Ⓑ Choose Send a Calendar via E-mail from the links in the Navigation pane.

3. Follow these steps to choose the date range:

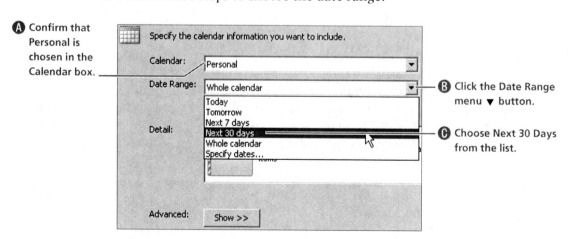

Ⓐ Confirm that Personal is chosen in the Calendar box.

Ⓑ Click the Date Range menu ▼ button.

Ⓒ Choose Next 30 Days from the list.

4. Click OK.

5. Follow these steps to complete the email message to send the calendar:

Ⓐ Address the message to the student on your left and your right, and to your instructor.

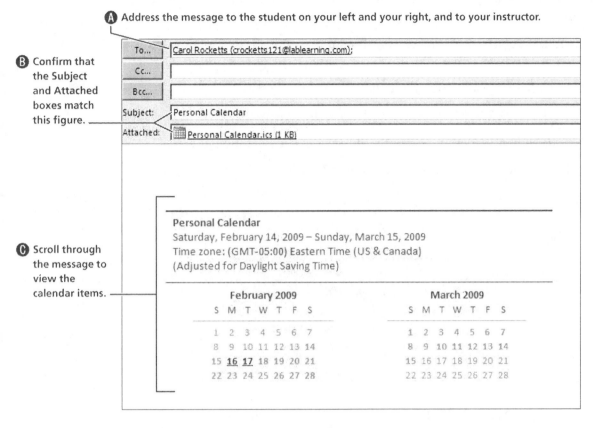

Ⓑ Confirm that the Subject and Attached boxes match this figure.

Ⓒ Scroll through the message to view the calendar items.

6. Click in the message box and type **Let me know what dates you are available for dinner**. Tap Enter and type **Thanks**.

7. Click the Send button.

Open a Calendar Received via Email

When you receive a calendar someone sends through email, it is a Calendar Snapshot. You can read it in the Reading pane, or you can open it as an Outlook Calendar. If you open it, it will appear on the screen next to your calendar. Or, you can overlay it on top of your calendar if you wish (this can be helpful if you want to see if there are any conflicts between your schedule and the one sent to you).

Hands-On 4.11   Open a Calendar

 If your computer does not have an email account set up, begin with step 1 below and perform the WebSim online. Otherwise, skip step 1 and begin this exercise with step 2.

1. Go to **labpub.com/learn/outlook07_fastcourse1** and click the link for Hands-On 4.11: Open a Calendar.

2. Click Mail in the Navigation pane.

3. Click the Send/Receive button to receive the new message.

4. Scroll down to read the calendar message in the Reading pane.

5. Follow these steps to open the calendar in Outlook:

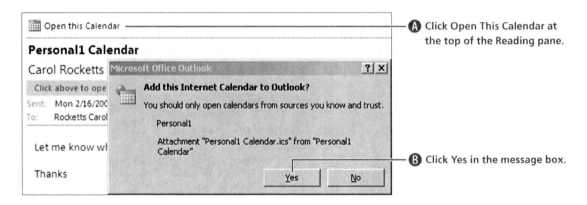

6. Click the Calendar button.

7. Follows these steps to view the calendars:

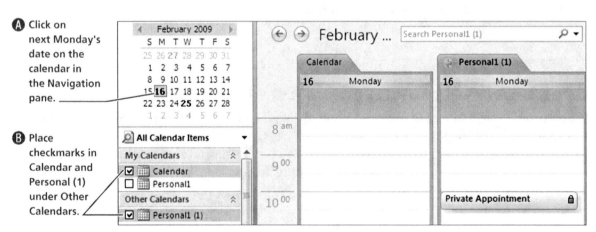

8. Scroll down, if necessary, to view the Doctor's Appointment.

9. Drag the Doctor's Appointment down to 12:00 PM.

10. Right-click on the default calendar and choose View in Overlay Mode.

11. Follow these steps to fix the conflict with the calendar items:

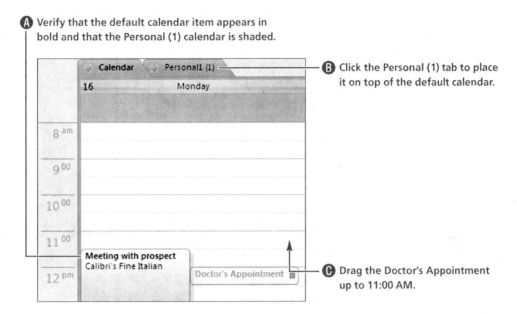

Ⓐ Verify that the default calendar item appears in bold and that the Personal (1) calendar is shaded.

Ⓑ Click the Personal (1) tab to place it on top of the default calendar.

Ⓒ Drag the Doctor's Appointment up to 11:00 AM.

12. Right-click the default calendar in the Navigation pane and choose View in Side-by-Side Mode.

13. Remove all checkmarks from all calendars except the default calendar, and then switch to Week view.

Printing Calendars

Calendars have many options for printing. For example, you can print a day, week, or month view. You can display or hide private items. Stef will routinely print her daily and monthly calendar to have with her at all times to avoid appointment conflicts. You can preview the calendar first to be sure it is the view you want to print. You can even print a blank calendar, which can be handy when you are just sitting down to think about next month's activities. To print a blank calendar, create a new calendar in a folder and print it. The following figure illustrates various print options in the Print dialog box.

Choose from Daily, Weekly, Monthly, Tri-fold, or Calendar Details print styles.

You can print a date range of calendars. For example, if you want a month's worth of weekly calendars printed, you can set the print range; otherwise, only one week will print.

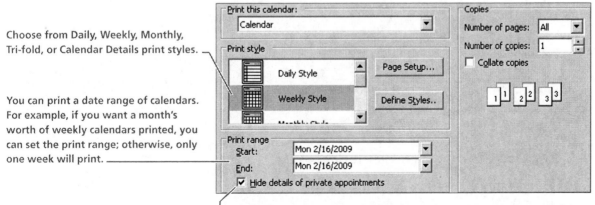

Check this option to hide the details of private appointments. Instead of the appointment details, "Private Appointment" will appear on the calendar.

Use Page Setup

Further options are available in the Page Setup dialog box within the Print dialog box. For example, you can set options to print the Week style in columns or from left to right, print only work days, and many others.

 Hands-On 4.12   Print Preview a Calendar

1. Choose File→Print from the menu bar.

2. Follow these steps to choose a print style and open the Page Setup dialog box:

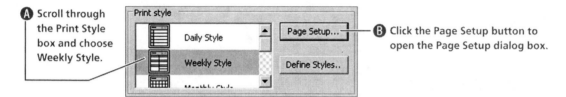

Ⓐ Scroll through the Print Style box and choose Weekly Style.

Ⓑ Click the Page Setup button to open the Page Setup dialog box.

3. Follow these steps to set formatting options:

Ⓐ Click the button next to Left to Right to print the calendar similar to what you see on the screen in Week view.

Ⓑ Place a checkmark in the box next to Only Print Workdays.

Options

Arrange days: ○ Top to bottom ● Left to right
Layout: 1 page/week
Tasks: No Tasks
Include: ☐ Notes area (blank)
              ☐ Notes area (lined)
Print from: 7:00 AM
Print to: 7:00 PM
              ☑ Only Print Workdays

4. Follow these steps to add a header to your calendar:

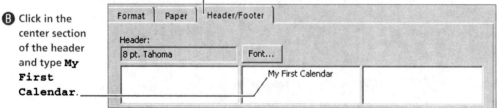

Ⓐ Click the Header/Footer *tab* at the top of the Page Setup dialog box.

Ⓑ Click in the center section of the header and type **My First Calendar**.

| Format | Paper | Header/Footer |

Header:
8 pt. Tahoma   Font...

My First Calendar

5. Click OK to close the Page Setup dialog box.

6. Click the Preview button. (If you are connected to a printer, you can click the Print button.)

Concepts Review

True/False Questions

1. You can undo the deletion of an appointment.   TRUE   FALSE

2. An appointment is a time period you block off of your calendar.   TRUE   FALSE

3. You can only create an appointment by opening an appointment window.   TRUE   FALSE

4. You cannot change the start date or time for an appointment.   TRUE   FALSE

5. Your daily tasks appear at the bottom of the calendar only when displayed in Day or Week view.   TRUE   FALSE

6. Recurring appointments can only be set to occur the same day and time for each week.   TRUE   FALSE

7. The Week view always displays the weekends.   TRUE   FALSE

8. Any item you have on your calendar can be marked as private.   TRUE   FALSE

9. Multiple calendars are initially displayed in Overlay mode.   TRUE   FALSE

10. You have three options of how much detail to display: Low, Medium, and High.   TRUE   FALSE

Multiple Choice Questions

1. How can you read a calendar that someone sends you via email?
   a. In the Reading pane
   b. Open it as an Outlook calendar
   c. Both A and B
   d. None of the above

2. You can print a calendar in _____ style.
   a. Weekly
   b. Monthly
   c. Daily
   d. Any of the above

3. What does the recipient see on your calendar when you have an item marked private?
   a. Nothing; the item does not appear on the calendar anywhere
   b. The words "Private Appointment"
   c. The appointment title only
   d. Title only with the words "Private Appointment" next to it

4. What happens to edits you made on an occurrence of an appointment if you later edit the series?
   a. The original edit to the one occurrence is lost.
   b. The original edit remains.
   c. You select an option to have it replaced or remain.
   d. None of the above

Using Notes, Tasks, and the Journal

In this lesson, you will learn about three very useful Outlook features: notes, tasks, and the journal. Notes are a handy place to keep those bits of information instead of having a messy desk full of sticky notes. Tasks are similar to notes, except that they have a due date, an option to remind you when the task is due, and can be assigned to someone else. You can also schedule time on your calendar for which to work on your tasks.

The journal keeps records of communications with your contacts. Journal entries can be entered automatically or manually.

LESSON OBJECTIVES

After studying this lesson, you will be able to:

- Work with notes
- Create and edit tasks
- Assign and accept or decline tasks
- Use the journal

LESSON TIMING

- Concepts/Hands-On: 1 hr 15 min
- Concepts Review: 15 min
- Total: 1 hr 30 min

CASE STUDY: CREATING NOTES, TASKS, AND JOURNAL ENTRIES

Josh Germaine attends a college whose preferred method of communication between students and professors is Microsoft Outlook. Josh has been using the email feature for a long time, but he has never ventured out to explore notes and tasks until now. He learns that he can keep his schedule handy by creating a note and leaving it on his Desktop for easy reference. One of his professors has already notified the class that she will issue assignments via Outlook tasks. Josh soon learns that he can also keep track of all communications with each professor and project team members using the journal.

Working with Notes

Notes are used to record miscellaneous information you would like to save for future reference. For example, you may want to save a list of all the usernames and passwords you use, quick reminders, or in Josh's case, maybe a little "cheat sheet" of possible test questions. In addition to viewing your notes in Notes view, you can put them on your Desktop and view them after you close Outlook.

Creating a Note

When you create a note, it is stored in a special Notes folder already existing in Outlook's Personal Folders. A new note opens a small box that resembles a yellow sticky note, in which you type your text. You must display the Notes view to edit or delete a note.

You can simply begin typing in the note box.

The date and time that you create the note are recorded.

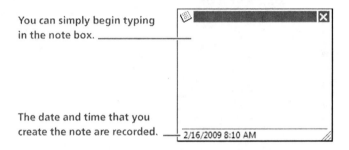

2/16/2009 8:10 AM

Copy a Note onto the Desktop

A convenient place to display a note is on your computer's Desktop. The note is always accessible. Simply double-click on it to open it while leaving Outlook closed. A note appears as an icon when placed on the Desktop. Since the icon is only a copy of the note, if you delete it, the actual note still remains in the Notes folder in Outlook.

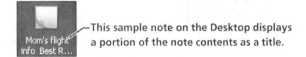

This sample note on the Desktop displays a portion of the note contents as a title.

 Hands-On 5.1   **Create a Note**

1. Click the Maximize [ ] button to maximize the Outlook window, if necessary.

2. Click the New menu ▾ button and choose Note from the list.

3. Type the following note in the Note window:
   Mom's flight info: Best Run Air, Flight 1279, 2:10pm, 12/20.

4. Click the Close ☒ button on the note.

5. Follow these steps to open and edit the note:

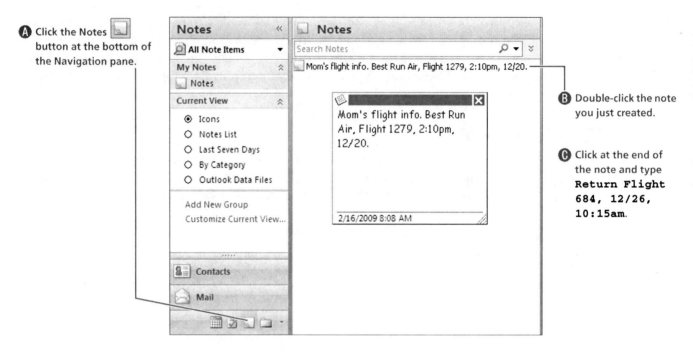

A Click the Notes button at the bottom of the Navigation pane.

B Double-click the note you just created.

C Click at the end of the note and type **Return Flight 684, 12/26, 10:15am.**

6. Click the Close ✖ button to close the note.

7. Click the Restore ⬜ button on the Outlook window to restore its size so you can also see a portion of the Desktop.

8. Follow these steps to copy the note onto the Desktop:

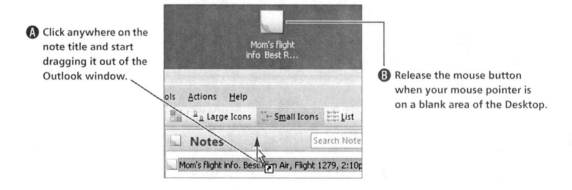

A Click anywhere on the note title and start dragging it out of the Outlook window.

B Release the mouse button when your mouse pointer is on a blank area of the Desktop.

9. Double-click the note icon on the Desktop and read the note.

10. Click the Close ✖ button to close the note.

11. Click the Maximize ⬜ button to maximize the Outlook window.

Working with Tasks

Tasks appear in your To-Do List and contain due dates. You can set options such as a reminder, notes, or the task status. You can assign a task to others, and likewise, others can assign tasks to you. When you receive a task, you can accept or decline it. Josh will probably accept all tasks assigned by his professor. The task window below details some of the options available for a task.

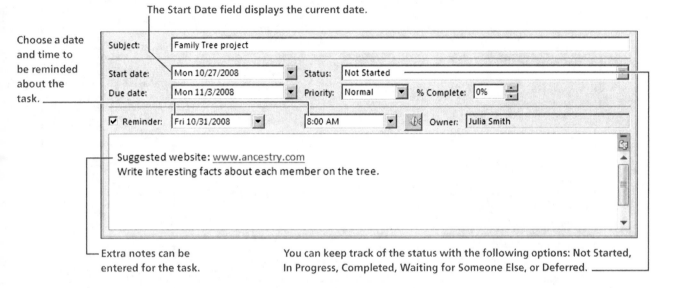

The Start Date field displays the current date.

Choose a date and time to be reminded about the task.

Extra notes can be entered for the task.

You can keep track of the status with the following options: Not Started, In Progress, Completed, Waiting for Someone Else, or Deferred.

Navigating Tasks

The list of task views is displayed by choosing Tasks from the Navigation pane. There are several ways to view your task list; the default is by To-Do List with the Reading pane situated on the right. When you double-click on the Type a New Task box, a separate task window opens for you to create your task.

Task Views

There are many views from which to choose how to display your task list. For example, By Person Responsible groups tasks for each person so it is quick to look down the task list and see who is doing what.

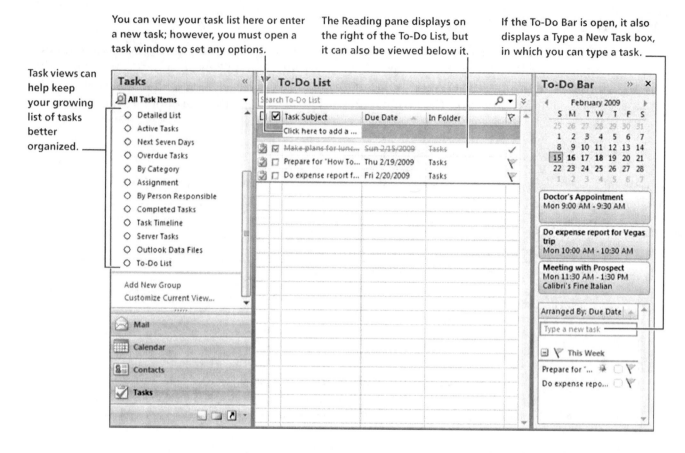

You can view your task list here or enter a new task; however, you must open a task window to set any options.

The Reading pane displays on the right of the To-Do List, but it can also be viewed below it.

If the To-Do Bar is open, it also displays a Type a New Task box, in which you can type a task.

Task views can help keep your growing list of tasks better organized.

Creating a Task

Tasks are usually created in Task view. Outlook automatically sets the current date as the start date and the due date unless you specify different ones. When you create the task, it appears in the To-Do List and the To-Do Bar when you have those windows open.

Schedule Calendar Time to Work on a Task

When you create a task, you can drag it onto your calendar to schedule yourself time to work on it. While not mandatory, doing this simple extra step helps keep you from booking yourself so heavily with appointments that you end up not having the time to work on the task. Until it is marked as complete, the task follows you on the calendar from day to day as a constant reminder. On the date you mark the task complete, it remains on that day of the calendar as a visual reminder of when you accomplished it.

 Hands-On 5.2   Create Tasks

1. Click the Tasks [icon] button in the Navigation pane to open Tasks view.

2. Click To-Do List in the Current View List, if it's not already selected.

3. Double-click in the Type a New Task text box to open a task window.

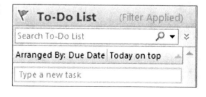

4. Follow these steps to create the new task:

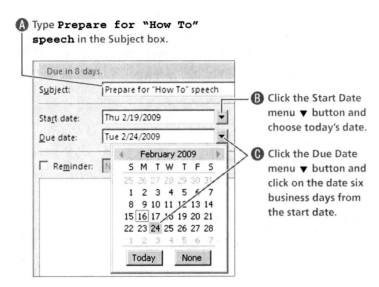

Ⓐ Type **Prepare for "How To" speech** in the Subject box.

Ⓑ Click the Start Date menu ▼ button and choose today's date.

Ⓒ Click the Due Date menu ▼ button and click on the date six business days from the start date.

5. Click the Save & Close button.

6. Click in Type a New Task, type **Make plans for lunch today**, and tap ⌷Enter⌷.

7. Double-click in the empty Type a New Task box to open a new task window and type **Do expense report for Vegas trip** as the task name.

8. Set the Start Date for tomorrow's date and the Due Date for next Friday.

9. Click the Save & Close button.

10. Click the Calendar ▦ button on the Navigation pane and click the Day tab at the top of the Calendar window.

11. Click on next Friday's date on the monthly calendar in the Navigation pane.

12. Click the Week tab at the top of the Calendar window to view next week's calendar.

13. Follow these steps to schedule time on the calendar to work on a task:

Ⓐ Click on the Do Expense Report for Vegas task you just created. (You may only be able to see a portion of the title.)

9 00			
10 00	Do expense rep		
11 00			
Tasks	Show tasks on: Due Date		
	Prepare ...		Do expe...

Ⓑ Hold down the mouse button and drag the task up and over to 10:00 AM on Monday to schedule that time out of your day to start working on the report.

Editing Tasks

You must open the task window to edit a task. Some edits you can make include changing the start and due dates, setting a date and time to be reminded, tracking the status, and adding notes to the task. Tasks disappear from the lists when they are deleted or marked complete; however, a completed task still appears in Tasks view with a line through the text. While there are many methods in which to mark a task as complete, the quickest way is to simply click the flag icon next to the task.

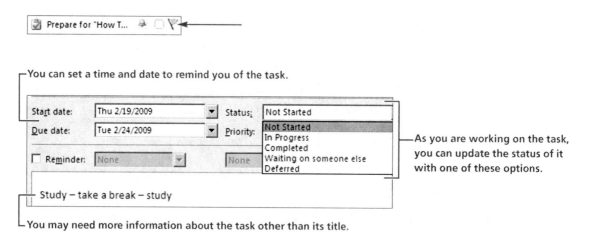

Set a Reminder

When you set a reminder for a task, a small window appears on the screen at the specified date and time. You can request to be reminded again in five minutes or up to two weeks, at which time the Reminder window reopens.

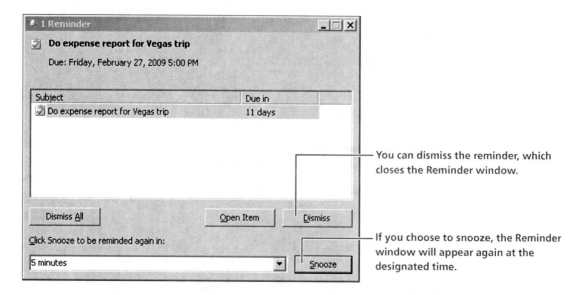

Hands-On 5.3   Edit a Task

1. Click the Tasks button in the Navigation pane.

2. Double-click the *Prepare for "How To" speech* task.

3. Follow these steps to add special notations:

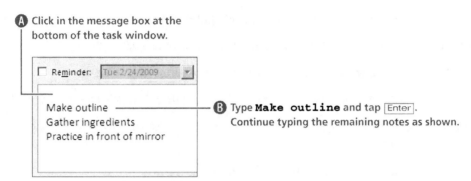

(A) Click in the message box at the bottom of the task window.

(B) Type **Make outline** and tap [Enter]. Continue typing the remaining notes as shown.

4. Follow these steps to set a reminder date and time:

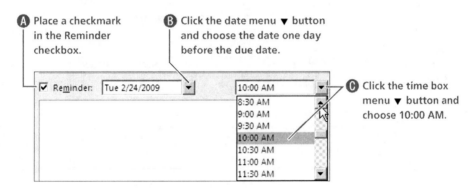

(A) Place a checkmark in the Reminder checkbox.

(B) Click the date menu ▼ button and choose the date one day before the due date.

(C) Click the time box menu ▼ button and choose 10:00 AM.

5. Click the Save & Close button.

6. Click the flag icon next to the *Make plans for lunch today* task to mark it as complete.

7. Click the Simple List view button in the Navigation pane to confirm that there is a line through the text.

Assigning Tasks

You can assign a task to someone or receive a task assigned to you from someone else. When you are creating a task and decide to assign it to someone, Outlook adds an address box to the task window for you to enter the recipient's address. After you send the task, you no longer own it; the recipient is the new owner. When the recipient receives the task, he or she can accept or decline it. As soon as a task is accepted, it disappears from the Inbox and appears in the recipient's Tasks list. You can also choose to keep a copy of the task in your task list and request to be notified when the task is marked complete. If you create a task for yourself and set a reminder, then later assign it to someone else, the reminder is turned off (because you are no longer the owner).

Hands-On 5.4 Assign a Task

 If your computer does not have an email account set up, begin with step 1 below and perform the WebSim online. Otherwise, skip step 1 and begin this exercise with step 2.

1. Go to **labpub.com/learn/outlook07_fastcourse1** and click the link for Hands-On 5.4: Assign a Task.

2. Click the To-Do List view in the Navigation pane, if necessary.

3. Double-click Type a New Task to open a new task window.

4. Type **Plan retirement party for Stan** in the Subject box.

5. Choose a Start Date for next Monday and set the due date for the following Monday.

6. Choose Task→Manage Task→Assign Task from the Ribbon to insert an addressee box in the task window.

7. Follow these steps to prepare to send the task assignment:

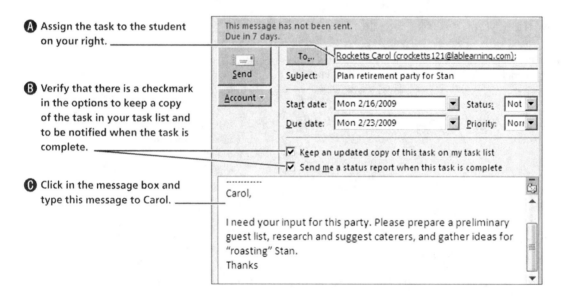

A Assign the task to the student on your right.

B Verify that there is a checkmark in the options to keep a copy of the task in your task list and to be notified when the task is complete.

C Click in the message box and type this message to Carol.

8. Click the Send button.

9. Double-click the *Prepare for "How To"* speech task and assign it to the student on your left.

10. Click OK in the box reminding you that the reminder has been turned off for this task, and then click Send.

Accept or Decline a Task

When you assign a task, the recipient has the option of accepting or declining it. If they accept it, you will be notified via email that it was accepted (and it appears automatically in the recipient's Task list). Recipients can choose to notify you if they decline the assigned task. Others can assign tasks to you also, in which case you will have the option of accepting or declining.

 Hands-On 5.5   Accept a Task

 If your computer does not have an email account set up, begin with step 1 below and perform the WebSim online. Otherwise, skip step 1 and begin this exercise with step 2.

1. Go to **labpub.com/learn/outlook07_fastcourse1** and click the link for Hands-On 5.5: Accept a Task.

2. Click Mail in the Navigation pane.

3. Click the Send/Receive button.

4. Click View→Reading Pane ▸→Bottom to display the Reading Pane below the Inbox.

5. Follow these steps to accept the task:

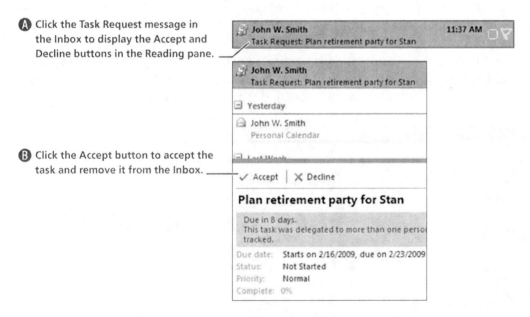

A Click the Task Request message in the Inbox to display the Accept and Decline buttons in the Reading pane.

B Click the Accept button to accept the task and remove it from the Inbox.

6. Click Tasks in the Navigation pane to verify that the accepted task has been added to the task list.

7. Choose the By Person Responsible view.

Using the Journal

The journal contains a record of activities you choose to track that are related to specific contacts. For example, you may want to track all email messages between you and your boss. This can be a very helpful feature, having a complete record of all communications with selected contacts. In addition to selecting electronic items to track, you can create manual journal entries to remember such things as phone conversations.

Setting Journal Options

The Journal feature is not turned on automatically when you first start using Outlook; however, after you turn it on and set the options, it remains on until you turn it off. You can set options to automatically record Outlook items such as emails, meeting requests, or task requests, associate them with certain contacts, and what should happen when you double-click a journal entry.

Recording Files Outside of Outlook

An option is also available to automatically record Microsoft Word, Excel, PowerPoint and Access files. For example, when you set Outlook to automatically record Word documents, it records any new documents in the Journal. Initially, the document is not associated with any particular contact; however, you can open the journal entry and choose with whom to associate it. The document appears in the journal and on the Activities page of the associated contact. Having quick access to documents relating to a contact can be quite useful. For example, if you prepare several documents for your manager, rather than remembering what folders you stored them in or what you named them, you can open your journal or your boss' Activities page and have all the related documents right there at your fingertips.

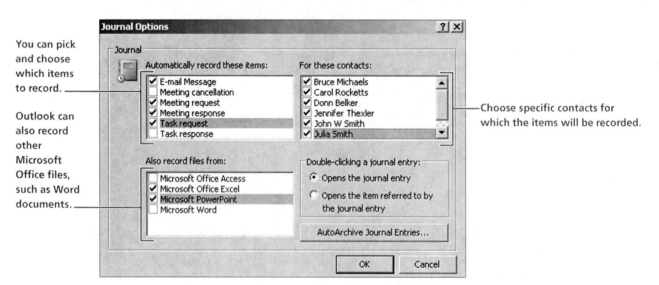

You can pick and choose which items to record.

Outlook can also record other Microsoft Office files, such as Word documents.

Choose specific contacts for which the items will be recorded.

Hands-On 5.6   Set Journal Options

 All students should perform this exercise as a WebSim. Begin with step 1 below.

1. Go to **labpub.com/learn/outlook07_fastcourse1** and click the link for Hands-On 5.6: Set Journal Options.

2. Click Tools→Options on the menu bar.

3. Follow these steps to set journal options:

Ⓐ Click the Journal Options button in the Options dialog box.

Ⓑ Put a checkmark in all items *except* the Meeting Cancellation and Task Response items.

Ⓒ Put checkmarks in the boxes for all of your contacts.

Ⓓ Put a checkmark in the checkboxes next to Microsoft Office Excel and Microsoft PowerPoint.

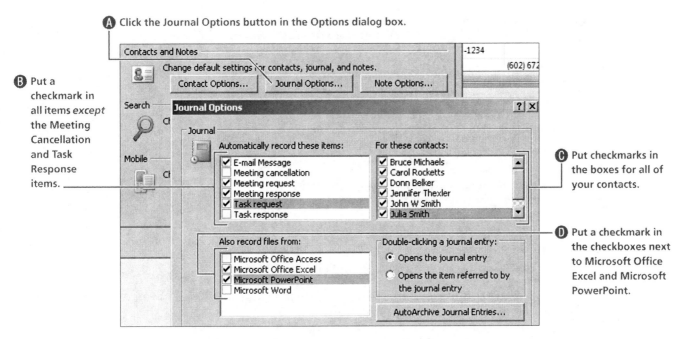

4. Click the OK button on the Journal Options dialog box.

5. Click OK to close the Options dialog box.

Create a Journal Entry

While the items you checked in Journal Options are recorded automatically for the specified contacts, there may be other communications that you would like to record. You can record other items such as phone conversations, meeting notes, faxes, and so forth by entering them manually in the journal.

All students should perform this exercise as a WebSim. Begin with step 1 below.

1. Go to labpub**.com/learn/outlook07_fastcourse1** and click the link for Hands-On 5.7: Create a New Journal Entry.

2. Click File→New ▸→Journal Entry from the Ribbon.

3. Follow these steps to create an entry:

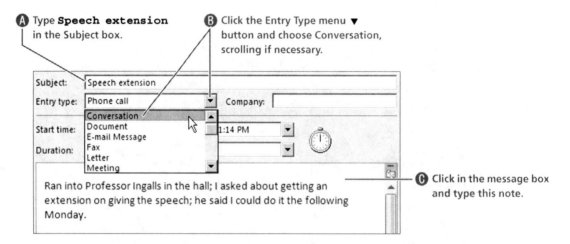

Ⓐ Type **Speech extension** in the Subject box.

Ⓑ Click the Entry Type menu ▼ button and choose Conversation, scrolling if necessary.

Ⓒ Click in the message box and type this note.

4. Click the Duration menu ▼ button and choose 5 Minutes.

5. Choose Journal Entry→Names→Address Book from the Ribbon so you can select which contact will be associated with this journal entry.

6. Click Bruce Michaels in the Select Names dialog box.

7. Click OK to send the journal entry to Bruce Michaels' activities.

8. Click the Save & Close button.

Viewing Journal Entries

Sometimes you may want to view all the records of just one particular contact. You can do so on the Activities page of the contact window. For example, if Josh wants to view all communications with his professor, he could open the professor's contact window and view the Activities page.

Activities page from within the contact window of a specified contact

Show:	All Items	▼	
📄 Subject ▼			In Folder
📑 Speech extension			Journal
📑 Prepare for speech			Tasks

However, you may require a complete view of all journal entries relating to a certain time-frame. You can open the actual Journal by choosing Go→Journal on the menu bar. This displays all of your entries in a timeline, which you can scroll through. The list can be grouped in several different views.

You can view the journal entries several ways.

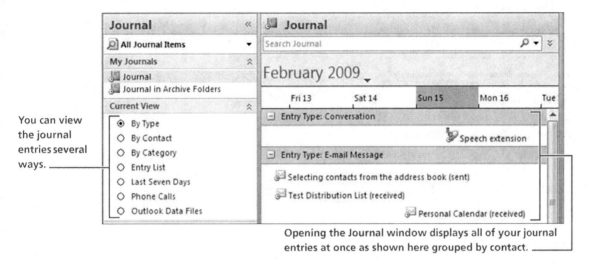

Opening the Journal window displays all of your journal entries at once as shown here grouped by contact.

Hands-On 5.8   View Journal Entries

All students should perform this exercise as a WebSim. Begin with step 1 below.

1. Go to **labpub.com/learn/outlook07_fastcourse1** and click the link for Hands-On 5.8: View Journal Entries.

2. Click Go→Journal in the menu bar to open the journal.

3. Follow these steps to open a journal entry:

A Click By Contact in the Current View list.

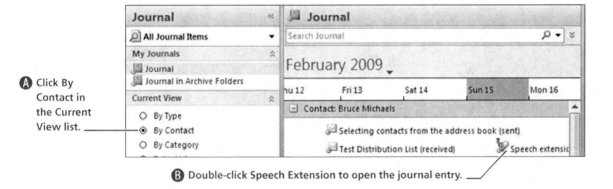

B Double-click Speech Extension to open the journal entry.

4. Click the Close [×] button to close the journal entry window.

5. Click Contacts in the Navigation pane.

6. Double-click Carol Rocketts to view her information in a Contact window.

7. Follow these steps to view Carol's Activities page:

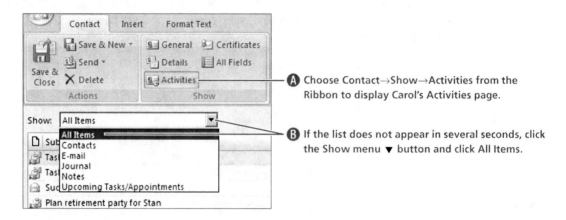

A Choose Contact→Show→Activities from the Ribbon to display Carol's Activities page.

B If the list does not appear in several seconds, click the Show menu ▼ button and click All Items.

8. Click the Save & Close button.

9. Double-click Bruce Michaels and view his activities.

10. Click Save & Close.

Concepts Review

True/False Questions

1. You can record Microsoft Word and Excel files automatically in the journal.   (TRUE)   FALSE

2. When you close Outlook, any notes on the Desktop are automatically deleted.   TRUE   (FALSE)

3. You can record a phone or other conversation in the journal.   (TRUE)   FALSE

4. When you assign a task to someone, you are no longer the owner of the task.   (TRUE)   FALSE

5. After you accept a task, it remains in your Inbox until you delete it.   TRUE   (FALSE)

6. Notes can be placed on Windows Desktop.   (TRUE)   FALSE

7. You cannot be reminded multiple times about a task.   TRUE   (FALSE)

8. A note can have a due date and a reminder set as options.   TRUE   (FALSE)

9. You can accept or decline a task assigned to you by someone else.   (TRUE)   FALSE

10. Outlook automatically sets the current date as the due date in a task and you cannot change it.   TRUE   (FALSE)

Multiple Choice Questions

1. What items can be automatically recorded in the journal for a contact?
   a. Email messages
   b. Task requests
   c. Word documents
   d. All of the above

2. Where do tasks appear?
   a. The To-Do List
   b. At the bottom of the To-Do Bar
   c. Both A and B
   d. None of the above

3. What options can you set for a task?
   a. Reminders
   b. Task status
   c. Special notes
   d. All of the above

4. Where can you view the journal entries for a particular contact?
   a. Contacts list
   b. Activities page
   c. Using View→Journal to display the journal
   d. None of the above

Index

Symbols
.pst data file for messages, 39

A
accepting tasks, 85
account, email, 15
address, email, 15, 18–19
All accounts group, 29
appointments (*see* calendars)
archiving messages, 39
assigning tasks, 83–85
attachments to messages
    printing, 34
    receiving, 30–32
    sending, 24–26

B
Blind Carbon Copy (Bcc) box, 18

C
Calendar button, 6, 55
calendars
    copying items to multiple, 67
    creating appointments, 55
    deleting appointments, 61
    displaying multiple, 67
    editing appointments, 56–57,
        60–62
    inviting attendees, 57–59
    options, 65–66
    overview, 3
    printing, 73–74
    recurring appointments, 59–62
    reminders, 57
    sharing, 66–73
    viewing, 62–65

Carbon Copy (Cc) box, 18
contacts
    creating, 44–45
    distribution lists, 49–52
    editing, 46, 52
    overview, 3
    searching, 46
    sending messages to, 47–49,
        50–52
    sorting, 47
    viewing, 43
Contents pane, 5, 6
contextual tabs on Ribbon, 9

D
date, changing appointment,
    56–57
Day calendar view, 62, 63
deleting
    appointments, 61
    messages, 38
Desktop, notes on, 77
distribution lists, 49–52
document recording in
    journal, 86
domain name, 15
due date, task, 80

E
email
    account types, 15
    archiving messages, 39
    automatic message check,
        16–17
    deleting messages, 38
    folder organization, 35–38
    moving messages, 36–38
    overview, 3
    printing messages, 34
    receiving messages, 16–17,
        29–32
    replying to messages, 32–33
    selecting multiple messages, 37
    sending messages, 18–28,
        47–49, 50–52
    settings, 15–16
    sharing calendars through, 66,
        70–71
etiquette, email, 18

F
file attachments to messages
    printing, 34
    receiving, 30–32
    sending, 24–26
finding contacts, 46
Folder List button, 6
folders, email, 5, 35–38
forwarding messages, 33

G
groups, sending messages to,
    49–52

H
help features, 10–12
Help menu bar, 10
Help toolbar, 10

I

incoming messages, 16–17, 29–32
invitations to meetings, 57–59
ISP (Internet service provider), 15

J

journal, 86–90

L

Login Information section, 15

M

meetings, managing with calendar, 57–59
Memo Style for printing messages, 34
menu bar, 5
messages (*see* email)
Month calendar view, 62, 63
moving messages, 36–38
multiple recipients of messages, 18

N

Navigation pane, 5–7
New button, 9
notes, 3, 77–78
Notes button, 6

O

Outlook
(*see also* calendars; contacts; email)
components, 3
journal, 86–90
notes, 3, 6, 77–78
screen elements, 5–9
starting, 4
To-Do Bar, 3, 5, 79–85

P

Page Setup dialog box, 74
panes, 5
Personal Folders, 35
printing
calendar, 73–74
Help topics, 12
messages, 34
private appointments on shared calendar, 66–67

R

reading messages, 30–32
Reading pane, 5, 7–8
receiving messages, 16–17, 29–32
recurring appointments, 59–62
reminders
calendar, 57
task, 82
Reply/Reply All options, 32
replying to messages, 32–33
Ribbon, 9, 23

S

scheduling
appointments, 55
tasks, 80–81
screen navigation, 5–9
Search box, 10
searching Contacts list, 46
security, email, 33
Send/Receive button, 29
sending messages, 18–28, 47–49, 50–52
Server Information section, 15
sharing calendars, 66–73
shortcut icons, starting Outlook, 4
signatures, 20–23
Snapshot, Calendar, 69–70, 71
sorting contacts, 47
spell check feature, 26–28
Standard toolbar, 5
start date, task, 80
Start menu, 4
subfolders, 5, 35
subject of message, 18

T

tasks
assigning, 83–85
creating, 80–81
editing, 82
overview, 3
reminders, 82
views, 5, 79–80
Tasks button, 6
time, changing appointment, 56–57
To-Do Bar, 3, 5
(*see also* tasks)
toolbars, 5, 10

U

User Information section, 15
username, 15

W

webmail, 15
Week calendar view, 62, 63
Windows XP, starting Outlook in, 4

CTC40 @ Conejo.tee.ca.us

ITEM: 1-59136-240-7
ISBN-13: 978-1-59136-240-1

9 781591 362401